DEATH BY COMFORT

How modern life is killing us and what we can do about it

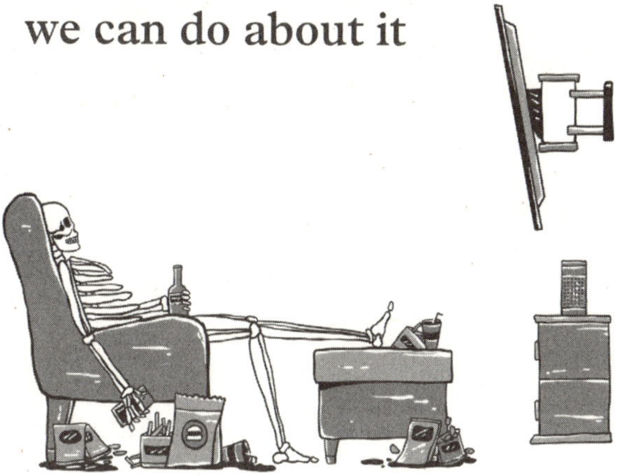

PAUL TAYLOR

MACMILLAN

Praise for *Death by Comfort*

I loved this book. For where we are at as a species, and also as individuals trying to navigate the beauty and mayhem of the human experience, it is the right book, with the right messages, delivered in an easy-to-understand language, at the right time. Paul is part educator, part coach, part terrifying drill sergeant and exactly what most of us need. This is an invaluable resource that, for many, will become an integral part of their new operating system.

Craig Harper, speaker, author, researcher, podcaster and PhD candidate

Many of us have been taught to avoid stress. In our most stressful moments, perhaps we have dreamt of escaping to a peaceful island where we can surf and lay in the sun all day. What if this attempt to escape stress is not the solution but the problem? This book shows that rather than avoiding stress, we can use stress to become stronger, more socially connected, healthier and smarter. The book is based on cutting-edge science, is easy to read, and is filled with clear insights and guidance.

Joseph Ciarrochi, professor of psychology and co-author of *What Makes You Stronger*

Paul has a brilliant ability to communicate science in an entertaining and engaging way. In this book, he expertly describes how the comforts of modern life are eroding our health and wellbeing. Get out of your comfort zone and use your human-evolved big brain to read this book. Although the science can get complex, the messages are not: eat real food, exercise often, get the right level of stress for you to feel motivated, challenge your body outside of your climate-controlled house to deal with heat or cold, build resilience. Apply the book's principles to your life and I'm willing to bet you'll experience the benefits.

Dr Joanna McMillan, nutrition scientist and accredited practising dietitian

In *Death by Comfort*, Paul has gone to the next level in translating bleeding-edge science into practices and tools that you can use every day to give yourself a life that is what you want it to be. Paul says what needs be said: that without unlocking the power of exercise, diet, sleep and managed stress, we can never be the best we can be. More than that, this book will ignite a debate around building a society that makes these things normal and part of what a health system should really do: keep us healthy.

Grant Schofield, Professor of Public Health and Director of the Human Potential Centre, Auckland University of Technology

I've always known Paul Taylor to be a master communicator. Then he wrote *Death by Comfort* and took that term to a new level. This easy-to-read book will truly challenge you to think about what's possible for your future self in all aspects of health. It will help you understand both the consequences of doing nothing and the incredible rewards of getting uncomfortable. You will learn, think and feel differently about how you look after that body and brain of yours. The people I care about will be hearing all about this book.

Lisa Stephenson, high-performance coach, author and speaker

Praise for *Death by Comfort*

To my wonderful wife Carly, without whom this book and many of my other achievements would not have been possible. To my 'princess warrior' daughter Ceara and my 'little Stoic' son Oscar, who are both a constant source of joy, pride and ikigai to me and Carly.

First published in 2023 by Major Street Publishing Pty Ltd

First published in India 2023 by Macmillan
an imprint of Pan Macmillan Publishing India Private Limited
707 Kailash Building
26 K. G. Marg, New Delhi 110001
www.panmacmillan.co.in

Pan Macmillan, The Smithson, 6 Briset Street, Farringdon, London EC1M 5NR
Associated companies throughout the world
www.panmacmillan.com

ISBN 978-93-95624-98-5

1 3 5 7 9 8 6 4 2

Internal design by Production Works
Printed in India by Gopsons Papers Pvt. Ltd., Noida

Contents

Contents

Introduction

Ancient bodies and brains in a modern world

'"You're okay the way you are" is not the right story. The right story is, "You're way less than you could be".'
– Dr Jordan B. Peterson

Imagine the history of the earth as a 24-hour period. The earth forms at midnight and spends the next few hours cooling down from a molten state. Oceans start to form and asteroid bombardments become less frequent. The first primitive life forms appear at around 4 a.m., but it's not until midday that the atmosphere becomes rich enough in oxygen to support the diversity of life that we know today.

At around 1 p.m., single-celled eukaryotes arrive; it takes another four hours for multicellular life forms to appear. The first aquatic animals don't come onto the scene until 8 p.m., followed by plants on land at 9 p.m. and animals around 10 p.m. Dinosaurs rule the earth for about an hour, arriving at 10.40 p.m. and disappearing at 11.40 p.m., likely because of asteroids hitting the earth and causing chain reactions that block out the sun and kill off many life forms.

Our ancient human ancestors split off from early primates at around two minutes to midnight, and us modern humans don't arrive until the last 15 seconds of the day! Then we get busy trashing the place and destroying our health.

Let's take a closer look at those last couple of minutes of earth's existence, from when the first gorilla evolved. Those two minutes represent around 6 to 8 million years of our early history, during which the chimp and human lineages split off from gorillas and the first upright human ancestor, Orrorin tugenensis, emerged. The first of our ancestors to live on the African savannah, Australopithecus africanus, appeared around 4 million years ago and had a brain size of around 400 to 500 cubic centimetres. A major milestone in human history occurred with Homo habilis – the toolmaker – appearing on the scene between 2 and 2.4 million years ago. Although it still had many ape features, it had a brain size of around 600 cubic centimetres and it traded some of the strength and power of its ape ancestors for dexterity and the ability to make tools, which gave it a competitive advantage.

Around 1.8 to 1.5 million years ago, our ancestor Homo erectus developed bipedalism – the ability to walk on two legs. This was advantageous because walking on two legs is a lot more energy efficient than moving on four limbs and is thought by many scientists to free up additional energy to develop a bigger brain, letting the brain of Homo erectus reach around 1000 cubic centimetres. There have been archaeological discoveries dating from around this time of the first use of fire by our ancestors, and this ability to cook food – both plants and meat – allowed us to unlock and digest a greater quantity of nutrients, giving us further available energy to devote to a bigger brain. Fast-forward 1 million or so years to 600,000 years ago and our more recent ancestor, Homo heidelbergensis, had a brain around the size of modern humans: around 1300 to 1500 cubic centimetres.

Around 200,000 years ago, Homo sapiens appeared on the scene and managed to outlast the closely related Neanderthals to become the prevailing human species. That 200,000 years is a blink of an eye in terms of the evolution of life on earth – it's the last second of our 24-hour analogy! But in that time, we have developed enormous capacities and made huge strides. We migrated out of Africa some 60,000 to 80,000 years ago and reached all four corners of the globe. The broad consensus is that language has only evolved in the last 50,000 years, and the 20,000 years since then saw the earliest evidence of rock art, musical instruments, fishhooks (which further assisted brain development through the provision of plenty of omega-3-rich fish), statues and woven fabrics.

Around 11,500 years ago, some of our species transitioned from hunter-gatherers to agriculturalists – a shift that was critical for the proliferation of our species because it enabled us to grow our population in sustainable ways. We later domesticated cattle, sheep, goats, chickens and pigs. We also 'domesticated' wheat and rice, giving us further certainty of food supplies, and we then learnt how to make alcohol for enjoyment. Around 4500 years ago came the earliest writing on stone tablets and papyrus, and the flourishing of ancient cultures in Egypt, Mesopotamia, Greece and the Indus valley. From this point on, many different cultures flourished throughout the world.

Here's the really important point, though. Up until this point in human history, we lived in highly stressful times. We had trouble getting enough to eat and were intermittently exposed to the stress of hunger, which got worse in winter months. We had to be highly physically active to hunt and gather, and that activity level didn't change much with the advent of the agricultural revolution – we know this because studies show that the Amish community, who live a traditional agricultural lifestyle without cars and modern technology, walk around as much as modern day hunter-gatherer tribes such as the

Hadza in Tanzania. We also spent all of our history to this point eating natural food sources in our local environment, including tubers, fruit, vegetables, nuts, seeds, and prey such as animals, birds and fish. The agricultural revolution added some greater certainty and provided the opportunity to make bread and drink the milk of domesticated animals (leading to one of the only changes in our genome in the last 10,000 years – changes in the expression of our lactase enzyme, allowing us to continue to digest milk and other dairy products after weaning), but we still ate local, natural foods. We went to bed when the sun went down and got up when the sun rose. We sat around the fire telling stories, passing on knowledge from one generation to the next. Everyone in the tribe or group had a role to play, and hence a sense of purpose and contribution, even from a young age. Life was hard and physically challenging, but we had strong, supportive tribal relationships to help us get through challenges.

The first and second industrial revolutions, from around 1750 to the early 1900s, propelled the human race to new levels of growth and prosperity, with invention after invention giving us the ability to expand our race and bring increasing levels of comfort into our lives. The third industrial revolution, often called the digital revolution, began in the late 20th century and involved technologies such as electronics, computers, telecommunications, smartphones, nuclear energy and the internet. Life expectancy has exploded, from around 27 years in the early 1700s to the low 80s in advanced nations now; as has the human population in that time, from around 0.7 billion people to 7.9 billion today.

However, not all of these advances have been good.

In advanced economies around the globe, we are now firmly ensconced in what I call the 'comfort revolution', where humans have massively expanded our ability to do two things that go against the current human genome when they're done in excess: the ability to avoid discomfort and the ability to engage in pleasurable activities. This is reflected in the shocking health statistics, which are getting worse:

- In 2022, 60 per cent of all US adults were living with a chronic disease, with 40 per cent having more than one.
- In 2018, 47 per cent of all Australians (and over half of all adults) had at least one chronic disease, an increase of more than 10 per cent in the last decade.
- In both countries, around 20 per cent of people experience a mental illness in any given year, and this figure is much higher for teenagers. It's projected that around half of the population in both countries will experience a mental illness at some stage in their lives.

These statistics are not unique and are mirrored in many developed nations.

Homo sapiens evolved and thrived because we could hunt and gather. Both involved high amounts of physical activity, and the ability to run for long distances meant we could hunt down prey with the tools we made. Modern science has clearly demonstrated that being highly physically active is necessary for the proper functioning of our bodies and brains, but most of us no longer have any requirement to do physical activity at a level more than the average sloth. We can change the TV channel, close the blinds, and ask Alexa to dim the lights and play music without having to get off our arses, and we spend more and more of our lives sitting down, often glued to screens. And that type of lifestyle ruins our physiology and, hence, our physical and mental health.

No longer do many of us have to worry about getting enough food, because there's now food available on every street corner and a host of new, flourishing businesses that will deliver almost any food we want to our door with a few taps of a smartphone. In many developed nations, ultra-processed food makes up 50 to 60 per cent (or more) of our diet. This food is a far cry from what our ancestors ate, and it's designed to hijack our brain's reward systems to make us crave more while making us fat and sick, as we'll see in chapter 4.

Exposure to cold and heat caused our ancestors to upregulate critical stress response genes, which made us more resilient; now, our thermoneutral environments are making us soft and contributing to our ever-expanding waistlines. For most of us, our mastery of indoor heating and cooling, coupled with amazing clothing, means that we never have to be too hot or too cold, which robs us of ancient mechanisms for adapting to our environments that have great benefits at a cellular level, which we will explore in detail.

We used to go to bed and get up with the sun. Now, we are destroying our circadian rhythms and sleep cycles due to artificial light and stimulating activities such as Netflix and social media. This screws with our metabolism in a mind-boggling number of ways, dramatically increasing our incidences of many diseases.

Our kids used to go through challenging rites of passage to transition into adulthood. Now, most are brought up on a diet of addictive, narcissistic technology, and mollycoddled to the point where they're not prepared for the real world and even moderate stress causes them anxiety.

We used to live in small tribal communities where everyone had a role and purpose. Now, we are digitally connected and physically disconnected, with few meaningful relationships and a chronic loss of meaning and purpose.

Society has 'evolved' to the point where we get offended if people have opinions contrary to ours, we attack them on social media and block them so we don't have to hear the counterargument. Many countries have ten days of paid sick leave that you're entitled to take, whether you're sick or not, and we can take a mental health day if we're feeling a bit off. We can now go to the doctor and get antidepressants or anti-anxiety medication to stop us experiencing negative emotions that are a natural part of life.

Opting out of negative experiences was not an option for our ancestors – and it built resilience. They had to be physically and mentally tough to survive in a dangerous, challenging world, which enabled us to exist today. A wide range of societal and technological advances have made modern life safer and less challenging, but an unintended side effect is that we've become physically weak and mentally fragile.

We are the most overweight, depressed, medicated and addicted cohort of humans that has ever lived, yet life has never been so good!

Clearly, something is wrong with modern life. We are ancient genomes in a modern world, and it's not going well.

This book explores exactly what's wrong and what we need to do about it.

Chapter 1

The good, the bad and the ugly of stress

'What does not kill me makes me stronger.'
– Friedrich Nietzsche

A lot of people just view stress as something that is bad, but scientists have revealed that the good, the bad and the ugly of stress is a better way of thinking about it.

My whole interest in this area came about when I was in the military. I was a newbie Aircrew Officer in the British Royal Navy and, like all Aircrew who could end up on the frontline, had to go through the Air 427 course, which was known as Combat Survival and Resistance to Interrogation Training. This involved ten days of pretty hardcore stuff, with a whole smorgasbord of stressors piled on top of each other in a cumulative manner in order to take us to our limit.

Firstly, we were exposed to cold stress for ten days, because it was in winter in the UK and we didn't have sleeping bags. We slept in what's called a 'tactical basha', a place where you would sleep if you were being chased by the enemy and wanted to stay hidden – basically, it involves kicking your way into a big thorny bush, creating a bed of dry leaves or springy ivy (if you could find either) and concealing the entrance. The course staff were kind enough to provide us with GORE-TEX bivvy bags (think a waterproof outer liner of a sleeping bag), so we didn't get wet, but there was next to no heat to be had from them.

We were freezing cold every night, and every day we would be exposed to lots of physical stress: walking for hours in navigation exercises, covering hundreds of kilometres over ten days. The first five days was a 'static phase', where we were taught survival skills while being physically softened up; and the second five days was an 'escape and evasion phase', where we would be hunted by a 'hunter force', which had dog teams and vehicles to help it hunt us. To avoid detection, we could only move at night, and we had to navigate to coordinates provided by 'secret agents' who we met every night. The only food they gave us for ten days was a chicken between four people, and it was alive when we got it.

The days and nights got progressively harder, with the cumulative toll of a combination of physical and psychological stress eating into our physical and mental resources. I managed to make it to the end and gave my name, rank and serial number to the guard, and received a Mars bar as a reward for completing the course. I was told to sit down in a particular spot before I ate my Mars bar, and I can distinctly remember almost peeing myself with excitement at the prospect of eating this Mars bar after ten days of no food, save for that quarter of a chicken. I sat down and, just as I was about to open my Mars bar, got exposed to what's called the 'shock of capture': a bunch of soldiers jumping me, roughing me up and then 'bagging and tagging' me – putting a hessian sack over my head so I couldn't see, and tying my hands behind my back. They then just disappeared, leaving me lying on the freezing ground wondering what the hell was going to happen next.

It didn't take too long to find out. One by one, we were loaded onto a truck, still 'bagged and tagged', and ordered not to speak by aggressive soldiers with aggressive dogs. When we were eventually all on board, we were driven for a few hours to a new location and taken off the truck one by one. No-one spoke to us – communication was all physical in nature. They cut my laces off my boots and retied my hands in front of my body. They then dragged me around by my thumbs until we stopped and they pushed me up against a building. The door opened and I was dragged into a room that had horribly loud white noise playing, like a super loud radio that hadn't been tuned to a station. I was put into a 'stress position', which wasn't that uncomfortable for the first minute or two but got progressively more uncomfortable and stressful. (Stress positions are very aptly named!) When I couldn't possibly hold the stress position any longer, I got a punch or a slap and was positioned in a different stress position, with the horrendous white noise playing constantly. And it was cold. And that's how I spent the next 12 or so hours. I thought I was alone, but we later found out that we were all in the same big, cold, noisy room together. The only 'breaks' that we got came when we were dragged out to be interrogated, which is not the most pleasant experience you could imagine, that's for sure! These professional military interrogators are true experts at messing with your mind.

Needless to say, the whole course was pretty damned stressful – physically, mentally and emotionally – for everybody who went through it. Despite that, most people found reserves that they may not have known existed, and most of us passed the course (but some had to repeat the whole thing).

Around a week or so afterwards, something happened to me that would normally have stressed me out – but it didn't. It was like water off a duck's back! And then another thing happened a few days later and, again, no impact. I began developing a theory, and I questioned other guys who'd been on the course to see if they had noticed something similar. Most of them said they too had noticed that stuff that used to stress them out no longer did. That's when I had my first aha moment in terms of stress and resilience.

This aha moment came to me because, before I joined the military, I had completed a master's degree in exercise science, so I understood that exercise is really only good for us because it's a stressor –the stress of exercise creates adaptive responses at a cellular level, which end up making us bigger, faster or stronger. That's when I realised that the same thing seemed to be occurring with psychological exposure. If you get through a period of psychological stress and you recover effectively, you can actually adapt and become better and more tolerant to stress. The military have a term for this: 'stress preconditioning'. For many years, they have conducted 'stress inoculation training' on soldiers to help prepare them for the inevitable stresses of the job. Stress preconditioning is also used in some medical procedures – an organ (such as your heart) is deliberately exposed to moderate physiological stress (such as reduced blood flow) before an operation to reduce damage to that organ in a subsequent operation.

What science has now uncovered is that exposing yourself to certain levels of stress of a wide variety of types induces adaptive changes at a cellular level, which can enhance your ability to deal with that stress. Recent research has also revealed a tantalising glimpse of a 'cross-transfer effect', which means the improved stress tolerance – to, for example, the physical stress of exercise – can carry over into improved tolerance of other stressors.

The military has worked out, through many years of observation, that the fittest soldiers seem to be able to handle the greatest psychological or emotional stressors. We now know that there is a molecular basis for that. Important proteins called 'stress response proteins' are released at a cellular level when we expose ourselves to any stressor – be it physical stress, cold stress, heat stress, nutritional stress (such as fasting), emotional stress or psychological stress – and these proteins activate cellular processes that not only help us recover from stress but also move us beyond resilience (the ability to bounce back) to become 'stress adapted' (we increase our ability to withstand further stress).

This is the whole proposition of this book: that we can move beyond resilience and not just bounce back but also become better because of the exposure to that stress, and that the process of stress adaptation can have spillover effects.

Let's now jump in and explore the good, the bad and the ugly of stress.

The good

The good part of stress is probably best summed up by my favourite philosopher, Friedrich Nietzsche, who famously said, 'What does not kill me makes me stronger.'

I'm sure you've heard of this quote (or a variation of it), but what you may not know is that Nietzsche was really talking about a process called 'hormesis' – although he didn't know it at the time. This branch of science is summed up by one of its leading researchers, Professor Edward Calabrese, as 'positive, stimulatory responses to low, subtoxic amounts of stress as opposed to adverse effects of high, toxic levels of stress'. Hormesis has long been recognised as a natural physiological response of biological systems to stress, and recent scientific discoveries have shown it to be a general biological principle at both the cellular level and the overall organism level. Hormesis has been shown to activate a cascade of cellular responses that slow the ageing process and enhance the resilience, health, longevity and reproduction of microbes, plants and animals by preconditioning them to harmful effects of stress. Essentially, hormesis makes you bulletproof – well, almost!

Here's an example: we know that physical exercise is a hormetic stressor. This means that when you repeatedly expose yourself to physical exercise followed by appropriate recovery, you become bigger, faster, stronger. A by-product of this adaptation to the stress of exercise is that you increase your protection against a whole host of chronic diseases. However, we also now know that more is not better. Numerous studies have shown that the impact of exercise on longevity follows a reverse J-curve: some exercise is good for you, and more is better, but very high amounts of exercise reduce the positive longevity benefits.

In another example of hormesis, the beneficial effects of low to moderate radiation exposure have been shown in a number of studies of plants, animals and humans. In human studies, groups of people who were exposed to levels of radiation previously thought to be dangerous actually suffered from lower levels of cancer in the following decades compared to their peers who were not exposed to the radiation. Examples include Chernobyl rescue workers who were exposed to nuclear radiation and British Medical radiologists in the 1960s and 1970s.

There are many, many more examples of hormetic stressors, some of which this book explores in detail, including heat stress, cold stress, phytochemicals in some foods, intermittent fasting, ultraviolet radiation from the sun and even alcohol! In fact, over 600 hormetic stressors have now been identified, and they all roughly follow the same hormetic curve shown in figure 1.1.

In physiological terms, this hormetic effect is referred to as 'eustress'. Eustress is stress that actually improves you – whether that is by making you bigger, faster, stronger, physically healthier or more psychologically resilient.

Figure 1.1: The hormetic curve

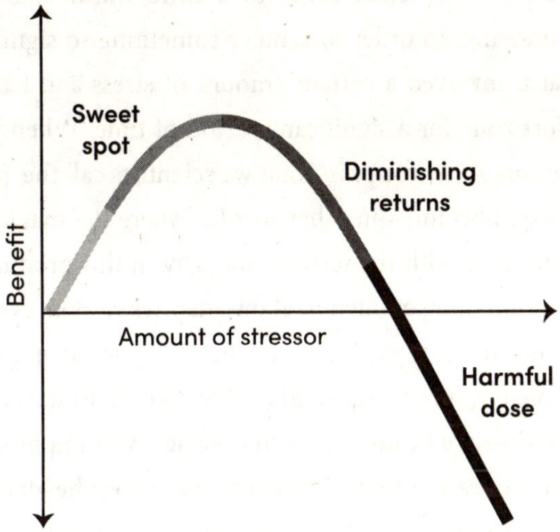

The science of hormesis is absolutely fundamental to the process of evolution. It allows us (and a wide range of organisms, plants and species) to adapt to a variety of stressors in our environment and not only overcome them but also gain some level of genetic fitness because of the exposure to that stress. Hormesis has huge implications for our health, longevity and even our achievements in life. However, it's becoming a lost art in the modern world due to the widespread availability of comfort.

Think about this in terms of your own comfort zones. Many of us prefer to spend most of our time in our comfort zone, but some people stay there for their entire lives! The thing is, comfort zones are a bit like the night hours after 2 a.m. – nothing really good ever happens there.

To illustrate this, think of a big achievement in your life that you're really proud of. Maybe you completed a degree or professional examination, finished a huge project at work, overcame your fear of public speaking, gave birth to a child, did an obstacle course, ran a half marathon or travelled alone to a third-world country to do some volunteering. In order to achieve something so significant, I'm betting that it involved a certain amount of stress and being out of your comfort zone for a significant period of time. When you're out of your comfort zone, you're in what we scientists call the 'productive zone of disequilibrium' – in other words, 'where the magic happens'. The key is to hang with the tension and stay in this productive zone of disequilibrium long enough to allow adaptive responses to occur.

Going back to the topic of exercise, here's a quick analogy: imagine you're completely out of shape and decide it's time to start exercising. Particularly if you're heading into middle age, you might jump back into an exercise session that you used to do in your heyday – let's say you go to a CrossFit session or a full-on personal training session. You get completely smashed by it, and you get home and say, 'That was way too hard, way out of my comfort zone – I'm not going back there'. You're clearly not going to adapt. It's only by starting an exercise program at the appropriate level for your current self and then continuing it, following the principle of progressive overload (where you increase the volume and/or intensity over time), that you'll adapt to become fitter, bigger, faster, stronger, leaner or more resilient. It's the repetitive exposure, staying in that productive zone of disequilibrium, that stimulates adaptation.

I talk more about eustress in other parts of the book, but this sums up some of the good parts of stress.

Let's now explore the brain and stress. Figure 1.2 is based on the work of neuroscientists Avis Hains and Amy Arnsten from the Department of Neurobiology at Yale University. It shows the performance-arousal curve, which is a new twist on something that has been around for many, many years. Have you ever done a really boring job? If so, what was your performance like? I'm guessing it was pretty crap, right? That's because your brain needs a certain amount of stress (we scientists call this 'arousal') in order for it to become interested in performing (but not too much, or we become overloaded). Stress follows the Goldilocks principle – it can't be too little or too much; it's got to be just right! When stress levels are just right, we call that the 'zone of peak performance'.

Figure 1.2: The performance-arousal curve – Goldilocks in the brain

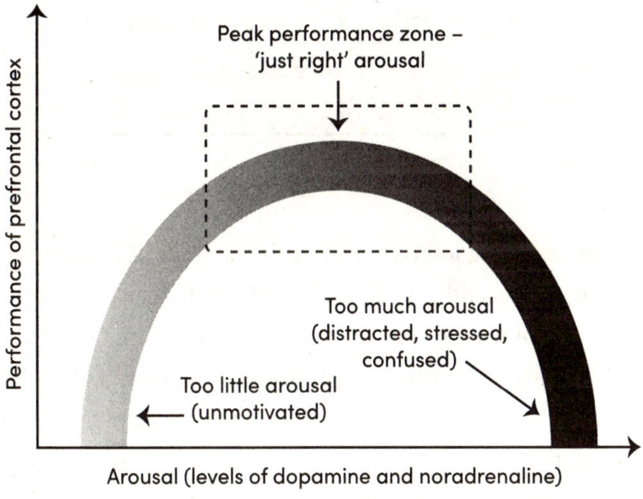

The optimal interaction between stress and performance occurs in what the psychologist Mihaly Csikszentmihalyi referred to as 'flow state' (see figure 1.3, overleaf). You go into flow state when you have demands placed on you, but you have the skills to meet those demands. Have you ever done an activity and been so focused you were not aware of the time or even your own thoughts, and you felt like you were in 'the zone'? That's flow state, and we need a certain level of stress (arousal) to reach this state of peak performance.

Figure 1.3: Flow state

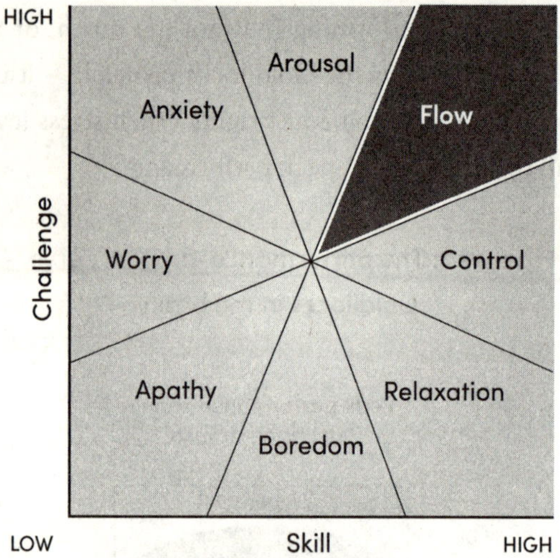

As you can see, the good part of stress has a range of tangible benefits for both your body and your brain. In addition to that, we have a deep-seated biological need for hormetic stressors if we want to reach peak physical and mental health, and optimise our longevity and healthspan (your number of healthy years, which is more important than your lifespan). Evolution drove us to seek comfort because it was not the normal state for our species, but today's world is filled with an abundance of opportunities for comfort that can make us fat, sick and mentally weak.

That said, not all stress is good for us.

The bad

I think we have all had times when we have experienced a bit of mental stress or anxiety – whether it's from having to do a public talk or an important exam, having too much work on our plate, being late for a plane trip or kids driving us up the wall. This is to do with the interaction between the frontal lobes of your brain (the rational, planning and judgement part) and your amygdala, which, among other things, is responsible for sensing and responding to stress or threats. Professor Antonio Damasio was the first to show that when your amygdala becomes sufficiently activated, it can actually secrete chemicals that block or dampen the activity of your rational frontal lobes. This process is termed 'amygdala hijack', but we all know it colloquially as 'losing our shit'! If you're in danger, this is an advantageous brain state – but if you're not in danger, it's definitely not where you want to be.

Professor Amy Arnsten added a bit more detail to this and showed that levels of arousal are predominantly driven by the two neurotransmitters dopamine and noradrenaline (sometimes referred to as norepinephrine). Think of noradrenaline as the brain-based cousin of adrenaline. When we are bored, levels of these neurotransmitters are low, but stimulation or arousal increases these levels. When levels of these chemicals are optimal (or in the 'Goldilocks zone'), this results in optimal cognitive performance, and an area of the frontal lobes called the ventromedial prefrontal cortex regulates the wild horse of the amygdala and keeps it in check.

Other parts of the frontal lobes are also on top of their game when levels of these chemicals are optimal. The right lateral prefrontal cortex is known as your brain's handbrake and is what inhibits you from taking inappropriate actions (such as punching your boss). We all have inappropriate thoughts, of course, but it's this part of the brain that kicks in to stop us putting those thoughts into action. (As an aside, you won't be surprised to hear that alcohol inhibits this part of the brain!) The dorsolateral prefrontal cortex keeps your attention focused and on task. Right at the top of your brain, the dorsomedial prefrontal cortex acts as your brain's simulator – this allows you to hold different bits of information together in your working memory, forecast into the future and make decisions. Hence, under the right conditions and with just enough stress/arousal, our frontal lobes are switched on and running the show.

On the other hand, too much dopamine and noradrenaline pushes us beyond the Goldilocks zone, and we suffer from amygdala hijack. Your dorsomedial prefrontal cortex no longer works well, so you don't think things through properly; your dorsolateral prefrontal cortex becomes inhibited, so you lose focus; and both your right lateral prefrontal cortex and ventromedial prefrontal cortex go AWOL, so your amygdala wrests control of your brain and you start acting like a three-year-old, and often say or do things that you later regret when your frontal lobes come back online.

That's the bad part of stress in a nutshell, and I think we can all relate to it.

The ugly

The ugly part of stress is when long-term chronic stress or distress has a negative impact on your physical and mental health, and the number of people suffering from long-term chronic stress is pretty sobering. A recent Australian Psychological Society survey showed that about one-third of Australians have a significant amount of distress in their lives and, at any one time, around a quarter of Australians are experiencing above normal levels of anxiety or moderate to severe depression. Similar rates of mental health issues are experienced by most Western countries.

There is now clear evidence linking stress and the development of both physical and mental health conditions. In addition to this, recent evidence has shown that chronic workplace stress has a negative impact on the structure and function of employees' brains, with reduction in volume in areas of the prefrontal cortex and an increase in the size of the amygdala (the part of the brain that senses and responds to stress or threat, remember). These changes mean that the brains of chronically stressed people become hypervigilant to stress – they are constantly scanning the environment for potential stress and threats. We see similar brain changes in anxious or depressed patients.

Workplace stress has long been known to drive a condition called 'burnout', which has been talked about in the research for decades. In May 2019, the World Health Organization (WHO) included burnout in its *International Classification of Diseases 11th Revision* (ICD-11), making it a recognised condition.

Also, never before have we experienced such high levels of mental health conditions around the world. At any given time, around 20 to 25 per cent of adults in developed nations such as the USA, the UK, Australia and New Zealand are experiencing a mental health issue, and the recent *Global Burden of Disease* study reports that, in 2017, around 792 million people globally were affected by mental health disorders, including 264 million people affected by depression and 284 million affected by anxiety. In addition, lifetime prevalence of mental health disorders – the average risk of developing one at some stage in your life – sits at around 50 per cent in most developed nations!

We all know that psychological stress alone can do pretty bad things. Interestingly, primates are the only species whose thoughts can activate the fight-or-flight response. This means that you can sit and ruminate about some bullshit that happened 20 years ago or an argument that you had last week, or catastrophise about something bad that might happen in the future or what someone could be thinking about you, and your brain will create a stress response as if you're being chased by a lion.

Take a look at figure 1.4 overleaf, adapted from the research paper 'The inflammatory consequences of psychologic stress' by Paul Black. You can see straight away that psychological stress can have really widespread negative effects.

Figure 1.4: The inflammatory consequences of psychological stress

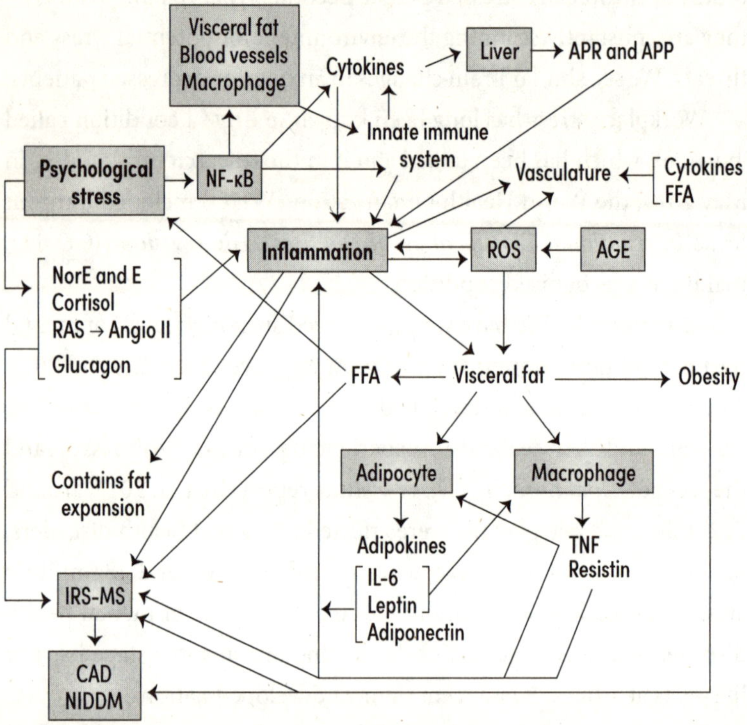

It's a bit of a spider's web, but if you follow the diagram from the top left, you can see that psychological stress induces a damaging biological chain of events. Psychological stress releases nuclear factor kappa bravo (NF-κB), which triggers the release of cytokines, messenger molecules that drive your liver to release acute phase reactants (APR) and acute phase proteins (APP). If you're thinking 'that doesn't sound good', you'd be right: these molecules sap your energy. They're also released in your body whenever you have a virus – they're basically the body's way of saying, 'Go and lie down while we sort out this intruder'. This is why people have low energy when they are chronically stressed.

All of this stuff drives inflammation at a cellular level. Cellular inflammation has widespread negative effects, including the increased formation of visceral fat – the fat underneath your stomach muscles and around your organs. As well as making you obese, this type of fat is very different to the rest of the fat in your body in that it actually acts as an endocrine organ: it releases adipokines, which are messenger molecules that are part of a feedback loop that drives more inflammation. That inflammation then forms more visceral fat, and so on. That nasty loop then contributes – along with the hormones released by psychological stress, such as cortisol – to the development of insulin resistance syndrome (IRS), metabolic syndrome (MS), coronary artery/heart disease (CAD) and type 2 diabetes (NIDDM).

Just looking at that picture is enough to stress anybody out! But it gets worse – scientists now know that chronic systemic inflammation contributes to a host of human diseases and conditions, as shown in table 1.1.

Table 1.1: Health conditions driven by chronic systemic inflammation

Disease area	*Health conditions*
Cardiovascular diseases	Heart disease, stroke, cardiomyopathy, atherosclerosis, cerebrovascular diseases
Diabetic complications	Chronic renal failure, retinopathy, sepsis, neuropathy
Chronic inflammatory disorders	Irritable bowel syndrome, psoriasis, chronic pancreatitis, chronic obstructive pulmonary disease, rheumatoid arthritis

Disease area	*Health conditions*
Musculoskeletal diseases	Osteoporosis, osteoarthritis, muscular dystrophy
Cancer	Lung, kidney, gastric, pancreatic, colon, lymphoma
Metabolic disorders	Fatty liver disease, heart disease, type 2 diabetes, sleep apnoea
Neurological disorders	Dementia (including Alzheimer's disease and Parkinson's disease), androgen insensitivity syndrome

That's pretty confronting, but if you can stay with me, it's important to discuss this last component of the ugly side of stress, which centres on how chronic stress manifests behaviourally.

To explain how this works, I like to use the analogy of a whirlpool (see table 1.2, on page 26), where the lower down you get, the stronger the downward pull actually becomes. Let's look at the different levels of this stress whirlpool:

1. We've all been at Level 1, where we feel just a bit out of whack. Your ability to concentrate and focus is a little bit out of kilter, you're easily distracted by your phone or email, your productivity drops a bit and you feel a bit more irritable.
2. This is where it starts to become more noticeable and problematic. Stress is affecting your energy, and low-level anxiety can creep in. Self-neglecting behaviours may also kick in: your diet starts to decline in quality, you don't exercise as much as you

should and you may start drinking more alcohol or even taking drugs. The stress is inducing behaviours that you know are not good for you, and you start to torture yourself. The 'tyranny of the shoulds' kicks in: you start thinking, *I should be eating better, I should be exercising more, I should reduce my drinking*, and so on.

3. This is where chronic stress starts to have noticeable impacts on your health. From a physical perspective, you're not sleeping well, and you seem to feel tired all the time. Your immune system is dampened, meaning that you're more susceptible to colds, flu and other illnesses, and you take longer to recover from them than you used to. From a mental perspective, you can develop significant anxiety and/or notice feelings of depression and a loss of vigour. Behaviour can become self-destructive, and you can slip into the habit of self-medicating with food, alcohol, drugs or gambling, because your brain wants an escape – it wants a dopamine hit to soothe the feelings of stress and anxiety, and so these behaviours go into autopilot. Deep down, you know that these behaviours are bad for your physical and mental health, your relationships and your career – but you just can't help it. You also start to withdraw socially, and this is a big warning sign.
4. The last level is burnout, which is characterised by adrenal fatigue or insufficiency. At this level, your adrenal glands, which have grown bigger due to the demands of pumping out excessive stress hormones, are now suffering from overload. They start to shrink and can't produce enough cortisol, which is important for normal functioning. Neurotransmitter systems start to burn out, particularly your dopamine and serotonin systems. The result is that the stuff that used to give you pleasure no longer does. You're not sleeping because of the low serotonin. The anxiety or

depression is now debilitating and, in the worst cases, a sense of futility and anhedonia (the inability to feel pleasure) manifests.

Table 1.2: The stress whirlpool

Level 1	Lack of focus, mindless multitasking, irritability
Level 2	Reduced energy, apathy, worry or low-level anxiety, self-neglect
Level 3	Fatigue, illness, sleep problems, moderate anxiety/depression, social withdrawal
Level 4	Burnout, severe anxiety/depression, anhedonia

When people get to the lowest level of the stress whirlpool, the road back is often very long and hard – which is precisely why early intervention is critical. Noticing the signs and intervening early can create a quick turnaround. The lower down you get, the stronger the intervention needs to be, because the downward pull gets stronger and stronger, just like a whirlpool.

Conclusion

Now that I've scared the crap out of you and given you all of the bad news, you'll be relieved to hear that the rest of this book is all about solutions, no matter where you sit on the whirlpool! It guides you through practical tools that you can use every day to get on top of your game and build your resilience to stress.

Before you move forward, just take a little time to reflect on the good, the bad and the ugly of stress. Does it resonate with you?

Have you noticed the effects – good or bad – in either yourself or people that you know?

Friedrich Nietzsche was well ahead of his time when he said, 'What does not kill me makes me stronger', but what he forgot to add on was, '... as long as I recover effectively and learn the lessons'. I explore the importance of that in later chapters.

Chapter 2

Mobilise your metabolism

'To keep the body in good health is a duty… otherwise we shall not be able to keep our mind strong and clear.'
– Buddha

If ever there was a magic pill, it's got to be exercise. For a lot of people, it's not fun; it can even be a chore. However, as we'll see in this chapter, science proves that incorporating more exercise (and movement in general) into your daily life can mobilise your metabolism and pay huge dividends for your physical and mental health. In this chapter, I also show you ways to make it easier to become more physically active.

In the previous chapter, I discussed hormesis – exposure to stressors, which at high levels can kill you but at low to moderate levels induce stress resistance. The single most important hermetic stressor that humans benefit from is physical activity or exercise. (I'll use these terms interchangeably for now but then dig a little deeper into the detail later.)

In my role as a corporate speaker, I have spoken to tens of thousands of people over the years about exercise. When I do basic polls of the audience, some people say that they are into exercise and some even love it, but many say that they don't enjoy it and lots do barely any exercise. Why? Mostly because it makes them uncomfortable.

My response to them is, 'It's supposed to be uncomfortable – that is precisely why it is good for you!' Physical activity is fundamental to our biology, and without high levels of it, we betray our genome. When we are physically active, we live in accordance with our genome, and we see the positive results through improvements in physical and mental health.

You're probably familiar with the idea that regular exercise can help to prevent or treat chronic diseases, such as heart disease and type 2 diabetes. You may have even heard that exercise may be helpful in the prevention and treatment of cancer. However, that is only the tip of the iceberg. There is now compelling evidence that exercise should be prescribed as treatment for 26 different chronic diseases and conditions, namely those shown in table 2.1.

Table 2.1: Chronic diseases and conditions that exercise should be prescribed to treat

Disease area	*Health conditions*
Psychiatric diseases	Depression, anxiety, stress, schizophrenia
Neurological diseases	Dementia (including Alzheimer's disease and Parkinson's disease), multiple sclerosis
Metabolic diseases	Obesity, hyperlipidemia, metabolic syndrome, polycystic ovarian syndrome, type 2 diabetes, type 1 diabetes

Disease area	*Health conditions*
Cardiovascular diseases	Cerebral apoplexy, hypertension, coronary artery/heart disease, heart failure, intermittent claudication
Pulmonary diseases	Chronic obstructive pulmonary disease, bronchial asthma, cystic fibrosis
Musculoskeletal disorders	Osteoarthritis, osteoporosis, back pain, rheumatoid arthritis
Cancers	Colon cancer, breast cancer, endometrial cancer, prostate cancer

As well as being an effective treatment for those diseases mentioned, exercise has been shown in separate research studies to help prevent many of them. If a pill could do all of this, it would surely be a magic pill. It's also critical, because some of these diseases – such as heart disease, stroke, type 2 diabetes and chronic obstructive pulmonary disease – are known as 'lifestyle diseases'. In the last 50 years, many of these diseases have become more prevalent, especially in advanced economies and, more lately, in countries where wealth is increasing, such as India and China.

The power of exercise to prevent or overcome depression

The last couple of decades have also seen rapid increases in psychiatric problems such as depression, anxiety and attention deficit hyperactivity disorder (ADHD), and the global COVID-19 pandemic has made things much worse. I believe that, even without the impact of COVID-19, deteriorating levels of physical activity have made a huge contribution to the increase in these conditions and, as such, the increase in these problems can largely be attributed to lifestyle factors. (In later chapters, I discuss how nutrition is also contributing to these conditions.)

You're probably familiar with the idea that exercise enhances your mood and your overall wellbeing. If I were to ask you why that is, like most people you may suggest that exercise releases endorphins – and you'd be correct, but it's not the whole story. Exercise also releases endocannabinoids. Both endorphins and endocannabinoids are important mood-enhancing chemicals.

Exercise also increases production of a bunch of neurotransmitters. This is really important, because neurotransmitters are responsible for communication between neurons. Without them, your brain doesn't work; and if levels are out of whack, it can contribute to a range of issues, including depression, ADHD, anxiety, obsessive-compulsive disorder and schizophrenia. Some of the neurotransmitters that exercise positively affects are monoamines – there are three of them, and they affect the following areas:

1. *Mood and sleep:* Serotonin, which most people have heard of, is really important for not just your mood but also your sleep – and, as you will find out later in this book, sleep and mood are intimately connected.
2. *Motivation:* Dopamine is important for movement but also anticipation, goal-directed behaviour and motivation. (I talk about the importance of that dopamine-driven motivation later in the book.)
3. *Managing stress:* Noradrenaline (also called norepinephrine) is another important mood-enhancing chemical, and also helps us deal better with stress.

There are two major classes of antidepressant drugs: SSRIs (selective serotonin reuptake inhibitors) and SNRIs (selective noradrenaline reuptake inhibitors). Essentially, these drugs make the serotonin and noradrenaline that you've already produced more effective, which can help mood in some people, mostly in the short term.

However, these pills are not the magic pills. Exercise is actually the magic pill, because (among other things) it increases the production of these neurotransmitters, which is more impactful than what these drugs can achieve.

A 2016 meta-analysis (which combines the results of multiple studies, giving us the strongest form of evidence) published in the *Journal of Psychiatric Research* concluded that 'exercise had a large and significant effect on depression', and the researchers suggested that their data 'strongly support the claim that exercise is an evidence-based treatment for depression'.

Exercise is also beneficial for people suffering from anxiety and stress-related disorders. A further meta-analysis published in 2017 in the same journal concluded that 'exercise is effective in improving anxiety symptoms in people with a current diagnosis of anxiety and/or stress-related disorders'.

Not only does exercise have a positive effect on mood, but it also has widespread and cascading positive impacts throughout the brain and central nervous system, and on your endocrine system, which regulates your hormones. Research shows that no matter what type of exercise you choose, it has positive impacts on cognitive, emotional, motivational, executive and motor control areas of the brain. It helps your energy balance, your immune control and your gastrointestinal control. It helps repair cells, and even creates brand spanking new brain cells and connections between brain cells! It also improves the structure and function of areas of the brain associated with willpower and self-control, which can help us to improve our choices around nutrition and lifestyle, thus reducing our risk of a whole host of chronic diseases.

Let's dive deeper into the science.

The science behind the benefits of exercise

So, why is exercise capable of all these diverse benefits?

The first clue to understanding this is that, for the average human, skeletal muscle is the single largest tissue type in the human body. The 640 or so muscles account for between 40 and 50 per cent of the total body weight of people who are not overweight or obese. Skeletal muscle has a huge capacity to adjust its make-up to meet the acute or chronic demands placed on it – this process is called 'plasticity'.

You may know that a well-designed resistance training program will increase the size and strength of your muscles, and that an endurance training program will enhance your ability to run long distances. These are both examples of positive (or adaptive) plasticity, but it can work the other way, too. Around one-third of skeletal muscle in an immobilised limb can disappear within weeks. This is an extreme example, but adults lose muscle mass at a rate between 3 and 8 per cent per decade, and it's not unusual for a 75 year old to have lost 50 per cent of their overall muscle mass since their twenties. Use it or lose it! You have probably experienced noticeable changes in your fitness when you don't exercise for a while, and as we age it gets harder to regain those fitness levels.

However, it's not just changes in the strength and physical capabilities of your muscles that occur through exercise or inactivity; profound impacts also occur at a cellular, organ and systemic level, because exercise is a very powerful regulator of gene expression.

In 2005, the legendary University of Missouri Professor Frank Booth and his team found that every time you exercise, there's a 'triphasic response' of your genes – that's three positive waves of gene expression changes:

1. *Stress response genes:* The first wave occurs after you have started exercise and is characterised by a rapid increase in – unsurprisingly – stress response genes! These genes, and their associated stress response pathways, are fundamental to the process of hormesis (the good stress), and a subclass of stress response genes called 'heat shock proteins' has really beneficial cellular effects. They get released inside your cells when you exercise, and they look for damaged proteins and then fix them by bending them back into the correct shape. How cool is that? This is important work because damaged proteins often trigger the cell to become dysfunctional or diseased. I like to think of these heat shock proteins as the cellular agents of resilience.
2. *Metabolic priority genes:* The second wave occurs when metabolic priority genes respond to particular metabolic stresses induced by exercise, such as low blood glucose. These genes help ensure that important areas of the body, such as the brain, still receive an energy supply even when your muscles are running out of glucose and glycogen. In the long term, the activation of these genes helps to improve your insulin sensitivity and protect you from metabolic diseases.
3. *Mitochondrial enzyme genes:* The third wave is of mitochondrial enzyme genes. You may have heard of your mitochondria – they are essentially the batteries, or generators, of most of your cells. Damaged mitochondria drive premature ageing (think of the Rolling Stones band member Keith Richards!) and disease. Exercise helps repair our damaged mitochondria. We also now know that a certain type of exercise called high intensity interval training (HIIT) not only helps repair the damaged mitochondria but can also induce mitochondrial biogenesis –

a bit of a mouthful that basically translates to brand spanking new batteries for your cells!

Another critical finding from this research was that the positive effects of exercise on gene expression last for at least 24 hours. The practical implication of this is that if you have a limited time to exercise during the week (as most people with busy lives do), you shouldn't spread it over one or two longer sessions; instead, do five- to ten-minute workouts every day (or as many days as possible). That way, you get more consistent improvements at a cellular level. To compensate for the reduced time of these workouts, you up the intensity so that you maximise the 'bang for your buck'. (More on that later in this chapter, when we get to recommendations.)

Magical myokines

Since the work of Frank Booth and his team in 2005, our understanding of the cellular, metabolic and overall health benefits of exercise has advanced enormously. A number of research teams around the world have discovered a class of cellular signalling molecules released by contracting muscle that drive communication at a cellular level, not just within muscle but all around the body and brain – they're called 'myokines'.

Myokines are a type of cytokine – the collective name for the small proteins that play an important role in cell signalling. (Think of cell signalling as instructions that are sent within and between cells for the purposes of affecting their behaviour.) Even though they are small, they have massive health benefits. Myokines communicate with:

- the muscle cell itself ('autocrine functions')
- nearby cells ('paracrine functions')
- distant cells and organs ('endocrine functions').

Endocrine functions are really important for your health. When myokines enter the bloodstream and communicate with bone, fat, liver, pancreas, heart, immune system and brain cells, they induce a range of metabolic benefits.

Science geeks like me get excited about myokines not just because of their positive impact on health but also because their existence indicates that muscle tissue can no longer be perceived as a 'dumb' collection of fibres acted upon by the nervous system – skeletal muscle must now be viewed as a fully-fledged secretory organ, which is a massive change. I could write an entire book on the benefits of myokines, but here are a few superstar benefits:

- Myokines get into your bloodstream and improve how many of your organs function.
- They can help turn white fat into brown or beige fat by increasing the number of mitochondria. This type of fat burns more energy, helping you to lose weight.
- The myokine BDNF has amazing impacts on your brain, including creating new brain cells and synapses (connections between brain cells), and protecting brain cells from damage. It is released during both aerobic exercise and resistance training in relation to exercise intensity, with peak concentrations occurring around lactate threshold (that heavy feeling you get when exercising intensely).
- Myokines drive metabolic adaptations, such as muscle and bone growth and repair, improved immune function, and a healthier gut, liver and pancreas (reducing diabetes risk).
- The myokine IL-6 is responsible for the anti-inflammatory effect of exercise, which reduces abdominal fat and helps reduce the risk of a host of diseases.

- Myokines improve the function of your cardiovascular system and reduce your risk of heart disease, as well as Alzheimer's disease and other forms of dementia.
- Myokines also exert multiple anti-ageing effects, which is why long-term exercisers live longer.

The comfort revolution

I agree with the many scientists who believe the reduction in physical activity that has occurred since the start of the comfort revolution is the main driving force behind the dramatic rise in chronic (and preventable) diseases that we are witnessing. Since the start of the comfort revolution, we have seen big increases in cardiovascular diseases, but even greater increases in obesity, diabetes, inflammatory conditions, mood disorders, autoimmune conditions and Alzheimer's disease (and other types of dementia).

What most of us have failed to realise is that our hunter-gatherer genome, which has not changed significantly in the last 45,000 years, requires and expects us to be highly physically active for normal functioning – not *optimal* functioning, but *normal* functioning. When we're not highly physically active, we deprive our bodies and brains of essential myokines, which makes us fat, sick, depressed and anxious.

To really understand the impact of a lack of physical activity, let's use the analogy of global warming. Global warming is the result of pumping copious amounts of carbon dioxide and other greenhouse gases into the atmosphere over decades. It took 20, 30, 40 years (or more) for us to notice the effects of all the damage, and now we have noticed the effects, the amount of work required to undo them is huge. The longer we wait, the more work we are going to have to do.

For me, this is a perfect analogy for your own health. Both good health and chronic disease processes occur at an ecosystem level – your 30 to 50 trillion cells work together in harmony to keep you healthy or drive chronic diseases. When you don't move, there are widespread changes in gene expression and reduced levels of the wonderful myokines that I discussed earlier. Over a few weeks or months, this can cause you to have a sluggish metabolism, reduced energy, a slight expansion of your waistline and perhaps a dip in your mood. But if you have low levels of physical activity for years, it spells disaster for your ecosystem, and dramatically increases the risk of chronic diseases and disorders in both your body and your brain, affecting the health and function of your cells and possibly creating disease. Death by comfort!

Sitting is the new smoking

I want to make special mention of the effects of prolonged sitting. You may have heard the phrase 'sitting is the new smoking', and I don't think there's any dramatisation at all in that phrase.

As far back as 2006, two neuroscientists from the David Geffin School of Medicine at UCLA, Shoshanna Vaynman and Fernando Gomez-Pinilla, published a brilliant paper called 'Revenge of the "Sit"', which was one of the first to explore in detail the impact of chronic sitting on our physiology, and especially on brain function. They showed that physical inactivity directly affected plasticity of the brain, and that the reduced expression of the myokine BDNF (which I discussed earlier) was central to these negative impacts. Since that study, dozens of papers have expanded our knowledge of 'inactivity physiology'.

A more recent Australian study showed those who sit for 11 hours or more per day have a 40 per cent increased risk of a range of chronic diseases, compared with those who sit for five hours or less – 40 per cent! Many people's initial reaction is that 11 hours sounds like a long time to be sitting, but let's explore this. If you are an office worker, it's likely that you will be sitting for six and a half hours of the eight hours a day (assuming you only work eight hours). Let's look at the rest of the day, though. You probably have breakfast, and you likely sit for that. Maybe you commute to and from work by car, tram or train. You likely have lunch sitting down, and I doubt you eat dinner standing up. Then, after a hard day's work, you like to relax, probably in front of a screen of some sort, and for most people that's an extra couple of hours or more. It's pretty damned easy to rack up those 11 hours, isn't it?

What we now know is that a lack of physical activity is one risk factor for chronic disease, but prolonged sitting is a separate, independent risk factor. So, if you don't exercise much and you sit for long periods, you have two independent risk factors for chronic disease. Even if you exercise a lot, if you have a job where you do a lot of sitting, you still have a risk factor for chronic disease.

This knowledge is pretty damned depressing, I admit, but it helps to create guidelines for physical activity, which I will get into shortly. First, though, we need to explore some important research carried out on members of the Hadza tribe, who live on the fringes of the Ngorongoro Crater in the Great Rift Valley in East Africa.

The last of the hunter-gatherers

The Hadza are one of the last hunter-gatherer tribes on earth. At the time of the research, they were hunting and gathering at least 90 per cent of their food, which gives us a fascinating insight into what sort of lifestyle our genome has evolved to support. By studying the lifestyle of the Hadza, we can understand just how much physical activity our ancestors from tens of thousands of years ago would typically have done. Then we can compare it to what most people currently do and what we are recommended to do by various health bodies.

The first study, carried out by Brian Wood and colleagues and published in 2001, examined step data from 197 members of the Hadza tribe across a collective 200 days using GPS physical activity trackers. I like this study because many people nowadays have an activity monitor to measure their steps. The common belief of the 'magic number' of steps per day is, as most people know, 10,000 steps. But where does this number come from? Like many people, I assumed that it was based on academic research, but it actually came from a marketing campaign from a Japanese company called Yamasa to promote the first ever wearable pedometer in the 1960s, called a 'Manpo-kei'. There is speculation that this number came about because the Japanese character for 10,000 resembles a walking man and 10,000 is a lucky number in Japanese culture. Rather amusingly, it has become ingrained in our psyche and has recently been adopted by organisations such as WHO, the American Heart Association and the U.S. Department of Health and Human Services.

Despite the widespread spruiking of this number, very few people actually manage 10,000 steps a day. In a study of over 700,000 people from 111 different countries using smartphone data, not a single country's population got anywhere near 10,000 steps on average. The range was between 3500 (in Indonesia) and just over 6000 (in China).

So, how did the Hadza stack up? It turns out that Hadza women logged an average of just over 13,000 steps, and the men logged a whopping 18,476 steps per day. As an interesting aside, this study also reported on data from a Canadian Amish community, who live a traditional, pre-industrial lifestyle with no cars: the adult Amish women in this study logged 14,196 steps per day, and the men 18,425. This suggests it wasn't the agricultural revolution that caused our modern problems, but rather the industrial and comfort revolutions.

A major problem with just recording your number of steps per day is that it doesn't consider the intensity of the physical activity that you're performing. Getting out of breath and increasing your heart rate is more important than the number of steps that you take. That's why many government recommendations, based on expert advice, talk about performing moderate to vigorous intensity physical activity (MVPA).

The current physical activity recommendations for adults (aged 18 to 64) from the U.S. Department of Health and Human Services are 150 minutes of moderate exercise per week or 75 minutes of vigorous exercise (or an equivalent combination) spread over five days. The UK government suggests you do at least this amount, and in Australia it's similar – 150 to 300 minutes of moderate or 75 to 150 of vigorous activity per week, incorporating strength training on at least two of those days.

This is where the other study of the Hadza comes in, which was carried out by University of Arizona anthropologist David Raichlen and colleagues in 2016. I think this study is even more relevant, because the researchers used heart rate monitors and GPS tracking devices on a sample of 46 Hadza (19 males and 27 females) over four two-week periods to measure how much MVPA they typically performed. The combination of these devices meant that they collected data not only on how much they moved (via GPS) but also on the intensity of that physical activity. They used four different two-week periods because they wanted to capture data from both the dry and rainy seasons, representative of all year round. The average age of the Hadza studied was 32 years, with the youngest being 15 and the oldest being 50 years old. This gave a spread of ages.

So, how did they go? They blew the current US, UK and Australian recommendations out of the water, averaging 135 minutes of MVPA per day! That's 945 minutes of MVPA per week!

Since the vast majority of people in advanced economies don't meet even the basic guidelines (with many coming nowhere near), it's not hard to see why we're inundated with chronic disease. When you understand the impact of physical activity on our biology, and how little we move compared to what our hunter-gatherer genome is designed for, you start to understand death by comfort!

The researchers in this second study also screened the Hadza for cardiovascular issues such as high blood pressure and high levels of cholesterol and triglycerides. Their high levels of physical activity translated into cardiovascular health benefits as well: they had very low levels of high blood pressure and virtually no risky lipid levels.

I'm not suggesting that we all become hunter-gatherers again, but the knowledge of the physical activity patterns of the Hadza, coupled with the knowledge of exercise biology and neurobiology, provides a basis for recommendations of incorporating physical activity patterns into our modern lives so we can ward off death by comfort.

How can we fix this?

In order to do this through physical activity, I have three recommendations: be active, get fit and build muscle. Why distinguish between them, you might ask? Well, you can be active by doing lots of walking but never get out of breath or do any strength training. Likewise, you can be very fit from a cardiovascular perspective, but still sit a lot and not have a lot of muscle mass; or you can perform a heap of weight training and have lots of muscle mass and strength, but struggle to run around the block. While doing lots of steps is good, your cardiovascular fitness is strongly linked with longevity, as is your muscle mass and strength (and more muscle also contributes strongly to a better quality of life when you get older), so all three recommendations are important.

If you are thinking, *What dismal news* (particularly if you are someone who does try to keep physically active), there is help at hand.

To provide a framework for my recommendations, let me introduce you to the concept of the physical activity triangle, shown in figure 2.1.

Figure 2.1: The physical activity triangle

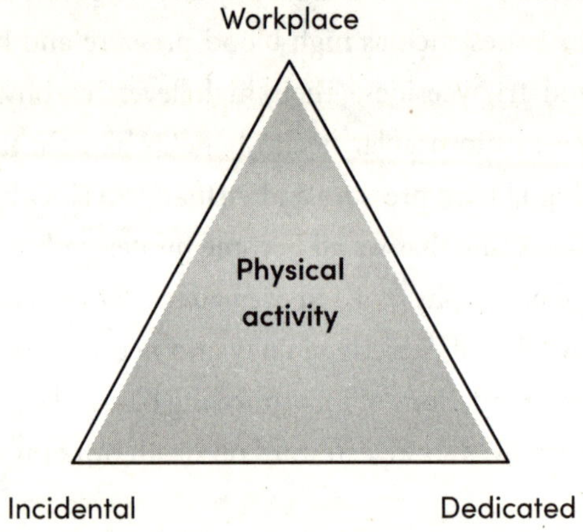

The three corners of the triangle represent the three elements that you really need to focus on here:

1. *Workplace physical activity:* how much you move when you're at work (or if you're a stay-at-home mum or dad, or not currently working, activity patterns during typical workplace hours)
2. *Incidental physical activity:* how much (or little) you move when you're not working or doing dedicated exercise
3. *Dedicated physical activity:* sport, exercise, going to the gym or running.

Workplace physical activity

Do a quick mental audit of how much you move and how much you sit in a typical day, and whether your sitting patterns are broken up or if you sit for prolonged periods. A lot of damage comes from sitting for 30 minutes or more, because this causes significant changes in gene expression. This can increase your blood pressure, reduce your ability to process glucose and affect your insulin sensitivity, among other widespread changes in your health. From workplace studies, we know that our levels of workplace physical activity have reduced by 100 calories (420 kilojoules) in the last 50 years. Some people think that isn't a lot, but that is 500 calories (2100 kilojoules) a week, which in a working year of around 46 weeks translates to 23,000 calories (96,600 kilojoules) – obviously enough to contribute to the accumulation of unhealthy layers of body fat.

If you have an active job, such as a trade or waiting tables, then you don't need to worry about this part. However, if your job involves a lack of movement and a lot of sitting, finding creative ways to boost your activity levels is paramount. Here are some options for you to consider:

- Stand up or walk around every time you're on the phone.
- Organise or suggest stand-up or walking meetings.
- Park your car further away from your workplace, or get off the bus or train a stop or two early and walk.
- Print at a faraway printer.
- Do a 'movement snack' – 30 seconds of exercise (such as a walk up and down the stairs) every 30 minutes or so.

Just getting up and moving every 30 minutes can undo a lot of damage, but aim to get out of breath. If you're working from home, this is easy – you can do squats, push-ups, burpees or sprints on the spot, or use kettlebells or some other piece of equipment for a short burst of vigorous activity. If you're in an office environment and feel a little self-conscious about exercising in front of others, you could walk quickly or run up two or three flights of stairs. Even 30 to

60 seconds of these more vigorous activities activates protective genes and increases blood flow and oxygen to your brain, while burning up stress hormones to bring our bodies and brains back to a natural equilibrium (called 'homeostasis').

Incidental physical activity

The same principles also apply to the incidental physical activity part of the triad. Remember, this is how much you move when you're not at work or doing structured exercise. It's important to note that when people do a lot of exercise, their levels of incidental activity tend to drop because they have expended a lot of energy. This is one of the reasons exercise alone is not an effective weight-loss strategy (the other being that we can also compensate by eating more).

Ensuring that you don't just flop on the couch with a beer or glass of wine after a hard day's work is important to your long-term physical and mental health. Reframing housework and gardening as opportunities to move can have huge benefits – not only can it give you a little extra motivation to do these tasks, but research shows that it can also have important benefits for your physiology and health as a result of the placebo effect. In 2007, Harvard University researchers carried out a study with hotel cleaners: half of them were told that their work met the guidelines for physical activity and were given examples of this, and the other half were not. Although their actual behaviour did not change, four weeks later the group who were told that information showed a decrease in weight, blood pressure, body fat and body mass index.

A good way to nudge up your combined workplace and incidental physical activity is to get yourself a physical activity tracker, such as a Fitbit, Garmin, Apple Watch or Oura Ring. A National University of Singapore study showed that people who invested in a fitness tracker increased their baseline movement by an average of 43 per cent, which is a huge improvement. I am a big fan of these fitness trackers because they help us get a snapshot of our lifestyle and how active we actually are – it brings to mind the old adage, 'what gets measured gets managed'.

I first purchased a Fitbit about three years ago when I started doing a lot of work with the City of Ballarat council (in Victoria, Australia). Everyone who came through my program received a Fitbit. I already had my Fitbit and was working on getting my baseline to 70,000 steps a week (because I, too, had been hoodwinked by the Japanese marketing campaign from the 1960s). When Gary (the head of HR at the council) got his Fitbit, he sent me a friend request and popped up on my leaderboard with 80,000 to 85,000 steps per week. So, the next week I increased my step rate to be just above his, and the week after that he increased his step rate to be just above mine. Over time, the competition between us created a new normal of over 100,000 steps a week. There's nothing like a bit of friendly competition!

Wearing a tracking device makes you very cognisant of the amazing number of choices you make every day around movement. Do I take the stairs or the elevator? Do I park as close as I can to the shops, or do I park further away to get an opportunity to walk? Or even better, do I just walk to the shops? Do I get off public transport one stop early so that I can get some movement in?

A typical office worker in the USA, the UK and Australia takes between 3000 and 5000 steps a day on average, which is pretty sad compared to what the Hadza and Amish communities. However, every little bit counts, so anything that you can do to nudge up that step count while reducing your sitting time will be very beneficial to your health.

Dedicated physical activity

If you want to fully offset the pitfalls of our comfortable lives and enhance your healthspan, a significant amount of dedicated physical activity is an absolute must. Remember those magical myokines that I discussed earlier? It's important to note that most of our myokines are released in amounts proportional to the intensity of our muscle contractions – this is what is called the 'dose response'. This is why running has more health benefits than walking, and lifting heavier weights is generally more beneficial than lifting lighter weights. Government health agencies around the world emphasise MVPA for this reason.

So, what does this all mean?

OK, let's get down to the nitty-gritty and talk about recommendations. It's both hard and inappropriate to give one recommendation for everyone, because we are all starting at a different base, and age does play a role as well.

Before we start, the big takeaway is that, unless you're already highly physically active, any movement of the needle in a positive direction is going to be a good thing. If you are using (or intend to use) a physical activity tracker, you'll get fairly substantial health benefits from nudging up your step count, especially if you're at the lower end of the range. A study published in 2020 and conducted on almost 5000 Americans over 40 years old showed that the participants who did 8000 steps a day had a 50 per cent reduced risk of dying of any cause compared to those who took 4000 steps a day. The dose response was again in play here, and those who took 12,000 steps a day reduced their risk of dying by 65 per cent compared to the 4000-steps-per-day group.

Walking speed also factors in significantly, because exercise intensity goes up as speed does. According to the Centers for Disease Control and Prevention (CDC), the range for moderate-intensity walking is 2.5 to 3.5 miles (4 to 5.6 kilometres) per hour and a brisk pace is 3.5 to 4 miles (5.6 to 6.4 kilometres) per hour or faster. Multiple studies have shown that those who walk briskly live longer, and a recent study from Dunedin in New Zealand reported that slower walkers had smaller brain volumes at the age of 45 than brisk walkers. That makes it pretty clear that slow walking is a lot less valuable than brisk walking. Walking speed tends to decline with age, and fitness levels obviously have an impact, so a better guide is to walk at a speed that gets you a little out of breath. (If you're fit, this may be hard to do, so just walk fast!)

Having a high step count (with brisker walking), and ensuring that you get off your arse regularly to break up prolonged sitting, pretty much take care of two parts of the physical activity triangle – namely, workplace physical activity and incidental physical activity. If you have a physical job or do a fair bit of moderate-intensity incidental activity (such as gardening or some types of housework), this can count towards your dedicated physical activity. Some of the more sophisticated activity trackers will register your heart-rate increases and count them towards your exercise minutes. It should now be clear that, while measuring steps is good, your major focus should be on MVPA – in simple terms, you need to get out of breath and exert yourself deliberately.

If you have a job that involves significant amounts of physical activity, I think that's a massive fringe benefit that's got to be worth thousands – if not tens of thousands – of dollars (or equivalent) of additional wages every year. Nearly 70 years ago, a famous study looked at the heart health of London bus drivers and conductors. It found that the conductors who walked up and down bus aisles continuously throughout the workday were much less likely to develop or die from heart disease than the drivers, who sat pretty much constantly while at work. A more recent study in 2017 compared postal workers in Glasgow (who were highly active) with their more sedentary office colleagues. Some of the office workers sat for more than 15 hours a day at work and home, and they had much bigger waistlines and much worse blood glucose and cholesterol levels than the postal workers, who walked around 14,000 steps per day. This study concluded that every hour of habitual sitting beyond five hours led to a two-centimetre increase in waistline and a 0.2 per cent increased risk of cardiovascular disease – that amounts to a 12-centimetre bigger waist and 1.2 per cent increased risk of cardiovascular disease if you sit for 11 hours a day, which most office workers do.

If you're not currently very active, making a concerted effort to hit government recommendations is an absolute must, and most guidelines now also incorporate some strength training. As a reminder, they are either one of the following:

- 150 to 300 minutes (2.5 to 5 hours) of moderate physical activity (you're definitely feeling it but can probably hold a conversation) per week
- 75 to 150 minutes of vigorous physical activity (you really struggle to hold a conversation) per week
- a combination of both.

Note that you should spread the minutes over at least five days, and include at least two sessions of full-body strength training.

The lower end of these numbers represents the absolute minimum that you should do. Hitting the upper end of these numbers consistently will give you a really good level of protection against a host of chronic diseases and positively impact your mental health, and give you about 75 per cent of the maximal benefits for longevity as very high amounts of exercise.

For a clearer guide to the intensity levels, check out table 2.2.

Table 2.2: Physical activity intensity levels

Effort level	*Explanation*	*Activity examples*
10: max effort	'Holy shit!' territory – I can only do this for 30 seconds or so.	1-5 rep maximum resistance training efforts, such as 30-second all-out sprints
9: very hard	Don't talk to me, I'm working my arse off!	Very heavy resistance training, some HIIT such as CrossFit, F45 Training, interval sprints
7-8: vigorous	I'm short of breath and definitely uncomfortable.	Most HIIT classes, fast cycling, running at pace, heavier resistance training, calisthenics, most competitive sports
5-6: moderate	I'm breathing heavily now and definitely working. I can talk, but not for long.	Walking upstairs, fast walking, jogging, cycling, circuit training with lighter weights, light calisthenics, more active forms of yoga, heavy gardening
3-4: light	I can do this for ages and am happy to chat, but I need to catch my breath every now and then.	Walking, golf, light gardening, heavier housework, light cycling
1-2: very light	I'm hardly exerting, but at least I'm off my arse.	Doing dishes or laundry, slow ambling, stretching

Survival of the fittest

Research shows that the most physically active group in middle age has a predicted life expectancy eight years longer than that of a sedentary group the same age, so there is a dose response to exercise, with an upper limit. What's also clear is that the single biggest predictor of longevity is your VO_2 max.

What on earth is this, you may ask? VO_2 max is the measure of your overall cardiorespiratory fitness, or capacity for exercise; for the layperson, a higher VO_2 max generally means higher fitness levels. Guides to improve your cardiorespiratory fitness have traditionally focused on exercising in different heart-rate zones, which are identified by the percentage of your maximum heart rate.

There are formulae for determining your maximum heart rate because it normally drops as you age, but they can be a bit misleading because not everyone fits neatly into them. However, if you're interested, they are as follows:

Males: 208.609 – (0.76 × your age)
Females: 209.273 – (0.804 × your age)

In order to improve your cardiorespiratory fitness, the usual recommendations are to spread your training time over the five heart-rate zones, which are:

1. 50 to 60 per cent of your maximum heart rate (warm-up and recovery sessions)
2. 60 to 70 per cent of your maximum heart rate (base fitness)
3. 70 to 80 per cent of your maximum heart rate (aerobic endurance)
4. 80 to 90 per cent of your maximum heart rate (anaerobic capacity)
5. 90 to 100 per cent of your maximum heart rate (speed training).

If you have all the time in the world to exercise, this can be really useful; but for those of us who have limited time to exercise, we need to get the best bang for our buck. It would appear that the best way to do this is to split your time between zone 2 (where you can still hold a conversation) and zones 4 and 5, which is very intense (an effort level of 8 to 10 from table 2.2).

Zone 2 is great for building both capillary density (think blood vessels) and mitochondrial density (think batteries for your cells), and gives you a good aerobic base, so I suggest one or two sessions of at least 30 minutes per week in this zone, depending on your fitness levels and goals.

Zones 4 and 5 are much more difficult, but the benefit is that they are a faster way to build your fitness. This is getting into the area of HIIT, and it's an intensity that you can't sustain for very long (intervals of up to 10 minutes in zone 4 if you're fit, and around 30 to 40 seconds in zone 5).

There are three different but effective protocols for exercising in these zones:

1. *Long cardio (for example, cycling, running or swimming) intervals:* Go at an intensity that you can sustain for around four minutes, recover for one or two minutes (depending on your level of fitness) and repeat for a total of three to five intervals.
2. *Short cardio intervals (HIIT):* Go at maximum intensity for around 30 seconds, then recover for 30 to 60 seconds, and repeat for ten to twenty intervals (depending upon your level of fitness and recovery).
3. *Short resistance intervals (HIIT strength):* Work for 30 seconds, recover for 10 seconds, and repeat for a total of 20 to 30 intervals. Alternate exercises so you don't fatigue a particular muscle group.

Table 2.3 (overleaf) outlines the exercise you should be doing.

Lift heavy shit!

Personally, I don't think enough emphasis is placed on strength or resistance training. As we get older, we tend to lose muscle and bone mass, which has negative (and often disastrous) consequences for our health. A 2021 systematic review and meta-analysis showed that between 30 and 90 minutes of resistance training per week reduced all-cause mortality by 17 per cent, which is massive.

I strongly recommend doing between 60 and 90 minutes of strength training per week, ideally spread over three sessions. If you are just after the health benefits, this can be all-body circuit training. If you can, incorporate squats, deadlifts and kettlebell swings – three of the best bang-for-your-buck exercises. If you're 60-plus, are just starting out or have any injuries, I suggest you see your doctor for medical clearance, and an exercise physiologist or corrective exercise specialist to get some guidance on a program for preserving muscle mass. See the end of this chapter for links to some video exercises.

Table 2.3: Exercise recommendations

Age range and goals	*Resistance exercise*	*Cardiovascular*
≤60, looking for basic health benefits	Minimum 2 all-body sessions per week of 30–60 minutes, or 4+ shorter sessions of around 15–20 minutes	1 steady-state (run, cycle, row, etc. at steady pace) session of 30+ minutes per week 1–2 interval sessions as described above

Age range and goals	*Resistance exercise*	*Cardiovascular*
>60, looking for basic and longevity benefits	2–3 all-body resistance circuit sessions per week, with balance training	1 steady-state session per week of 20+ minutes 1–2 interval sessions as described above (if cleared by doctor)
≤60, looking for peak health and longevity benefits	Structured strength training program 3–5 times per week designed by a professional	≥2 steady-state sessions per week of 30+ minutes ≥2 interval sessions (if cleared by doctor)
>60, looking for peak health and longevity benefits	Structured strength training program 3–4 times per week designed by a professional, with balance training	≥2 steady-state sessions per week of 20+ minutes 2 interval sessions (if cleared by doctor)

The total time spent exercising per week should be at least 150 minutes of moderate exercise or 75 minutes of vigorous exercise for basic benefits, and double those amounts for optimal health and longevity.

Note that you can combine the resistance training and cardio if you are doing a form of HIIT training that combines strength and cardiovascular training, such as CrossFit or F45 Training. Also, keep total exercise time across both types to less than ten hours per week, because any more may blunt longevity benefits. If you are into endurance sports such as marathon running, cycling or triathlon, you may need to exceed these recommendations to achieve optimal performance, but it appears there may be a trade-off between optimal performance and optimal longevity benefits – the jury's still out on that.

Movement snacks

I talked earlier about the shocking metabolic consequences of prolonged sitting. In addition, if you sit for significant parts of the day, it's crucial that you regularly interrupt that sitting to reactivate positive gene expression and mobilise your metabolism again. The goal is to get blood flowing and oxygen to your brain, so you should aim to get out of breath and get a muscle burn.

In addition to the exercise recommendations in table 2.3, I recommend people of all age ranges and goals do a minimum of six 30- to 60-second movement snacks per day to break up sitting. Examples include kettlebell swings (my favourite), goblet squats (with weight in hands), sprints on the spot, push-ups off the ground or your desk, burpees, squats or jumping squats, lunges, and kettlebell or dumbbell sumo squats.

Can I do too much?

The simple answer to this is yes – and this is often where passion for a sport or activity clashes with longevity benefits. The resistance training study I mentioned earlier showed that the longevity benefits started to disappear at levels over 100 minutes per week, and numerous studies into the impact of cardiovascular exercise show that you start to lose some of the longevity benefits after more than about ten hours per week of exercise. That said, you're still better off than people who do no or minimal exercise.

One problem that has surfaced in the last couple of decades is the significant incidence of atrial fibrillation (AF) in both professional and amateur athletes. It occurs mostly in endurance athletes, such as marathon runners, cyclists and triathletes, but it has also been found in elite rowers. It appears to result from having the heart rate at high levels for prolonged periods (a few hours) or at very high levels for shorter periods. I suspect that people who engage in a lot of an activity such as CrossFit, where the heart rate is at very high levels for an hour or so, may also put themselves at risk if they're nudging the ten-hours-per-week level of exercise. Young endurance athletes are especially prone to AF – no-one is 100 per cent sure why – as are people who have done these sorts of activities for many years.

It appears at this stage that high overall training volume with a significantly elevated heart rate is the culprit. Therefore, my personal recommendation is that, if longevity and healthspan are your goals and you want to do a marathon or triathlon, do a couple and then switch to something else – and keep your long-term total exercise time below ten hours per week. If performance in sport is your goal, that's a different conversation, but be aware that there may be a trade-off between optimal performance and longevity.

Conclusion

Many people's reason for exercise is to lose weight or keep slim, but it should be abundantly clear to you now that exercise is about so much more than how you look. It is about how your ecosystem of cells functions, how your brain and entire central nervous system functions and performs, and how that helps you make better environmental choices. These choices then reduce your risk of a whole host of chronic diseases and make you function at a better level.

Recent developments in our understanding of hormetic stressors have found that exercise actually drives cellular processes that enhance your resilience. When you go to the doctor for help with a disease or condition, they may prescribe you a pill. Think of this pill like a musical instrument that creates a particular sound. Using that analogy, every time you exercise you are activating an entire orchestra, and that symphony it's playing is sweet music for your entire body and brain. Boom!

Please scan the below QR code for some videos and further exercise recommendations.

SCAN ME

Chapter 3

Harvest discomfort

'We must undergo a hard winter training and not rush into things for which we have not prepared.'
– Epictetus

Many psychologists have studied tolerating discomfort, and there are many academic papers written on the subject of both discomfort tolerance (tolerating physical discomfort) and distress tolerance (tolerating psychological discomfort). There are even validated questionnaires dedicated to both topics, and it's been shown that people who score poorly on these are more prone to a range of psychological problems, such as anxiety and depression.

In this chapter, however, we're not going to talk about 'tolerating', which means to be capable of being subjected to something without an adverse reaction, because it is not a true representation of the critical biological concept of hormesis (which, you'll recall from earlier chapters, involves becoming stress resistant due to low to moderate levels of exposure to a stressor or toxin).

This is where 'discomfort harvesting' comes in.

Cold stress

First, we're going to explore something a little bit out of left field: cold showers. When I talk about cold showers, most people respond with 'Ooh, I don't know about that'. That's understandable, because it's not the most pleasant feeling in the world, but it turns out there are actually really good reasons why we should have cold showers – and not just occasionally, but every day.

A really interesting randomised control trial was performed in the Netherlands recently on the effect of cold showering on health and work. You may have heard that a randomised control trial is the best form of clinical evidence, because it's the best way of showing that the effects of the intervention are attributable to the intervention itself and not to the placebo effect (which can be very powerful). In this study, they took a bunch of volunteers and randomly split them into two groups. One group was assigned as a control group, and they were instructed to continue to have their showers as normal. The other group was the intervention group, and they were asked to have a cold shower at the end of their normal shower every day (so, they turned the temperature to cold after their normal warm shower) for either 30, 60 or 90 seconds (they were assigned to three subgroups for this).

The researchers measured their health, their sickness levels and their absenteeism from the workplace at the beginning of the study, and again after six months. Then they told everyone that the intervention period was over, but that they would like to do follow-up measurements after another six months. The guys who were having the cold showers were told that they didn't have to have them anymore, unless they really wanted to.

When the researchers came back at the end of the second six months, it turned out that at least 90 per cent of the people who had the cold showers chose to continue with them! That says something in and of itself. And when they measured their health, sickness and absenteeism, those who had the regular cold showers (for either 30, 60 or 90 seconds) experienced a 29 per cent reduction in sickness and absenteeism.

I think you'll agree that's pretty huge; in fact, it would be judged as a very successful workplace health intervention, and it cost absolutely nothing. Nada. The other piece of good news is that it turned out doing 60 or 90 seconds of a cold shower wasn't that much better than doing 30 seconds.

Other cold exposure techniques include cold-water swimming – which may or may not be practical depending on where you live – and cryotherapy, where you enter a special chamber and are exposed to extremely cold air for 1 to 3 minutes, with temperatures as low as −178°C (−298°F) – yep, you read that right! These chambers are few and far between, and typically quite expensive, and cold water is a more effective way of cooling your core body temperature than cold air.

In 2020, WHO recommended that we have cold showers for good physical and mental health, and scientists have uncovered why they're beneficial. What we now know is that whenever you expose yourself to cold, you activate the hormesis-driving stress response proteins. As it turns out, not only do you have the heat shock proteins associated with exercise, but there is also another class of proteins called 'cold shock proteins' that seem to have independent and synergistic effects to the heat shock proteins.

We also know that a myokine (those messenger molecules released by exercise) called Irisin is released in muscle whenever you either exercise or expose yourself to cold. Scientists have recently discovered that Irisin release produces beneficial downstream effects that protect our cells: Irisin can actually protect your brain cells from damage and increase the formation of new neurons and synapses by triggering the release of BDNF. This is obviously a good reason why we should have those cold showers.

Another reason is that you increase levels of noradrenaline (norepinephrine) in the brain. This is a critical part of the cold-shock response because it increases heart rate, constricts blood vessels, activates thermogenesis (heat production) and positively affects immune function. You may also remember from the previous chapter that this is a powerful feel-good chemical. This is why people who have cold showers actually feel great afterwards. 'Really invigorating' is the term that I often hear people use, and I notice this myself. Research shows that both two minutes of cryotherapy and 20 seconds of immersion in 4.4°C (40°F) water increase noradrenaline by 200 to 300 per cent.

Regular cold exposure has been shown to increase the amount of 'brown fat' that you have. Studies in animals and humans have indicated that brown fat can improve glucose and insulin sensitivity, increase fat oxidation and protect against diet-induced obesity. The 'browning' of your fat occurs because the amount of mitochondria in your fat cells is increased and your metabolic rate (the amount of calories you burn at rest) goes up.

In addition, your immune system gets upregulated when you are regularly exposed to cold water, which is why those people in the research study weren't getting sick as much as those in the control group. Scientists have also studied swimmers who swim all year round – which obviously involves regular swimming in cold water during the colder months – and they found that those people had better cardiovascular function, had better immune function, and lived longer than aged-matched control groups who actually do similar amounts of exercise but not in the cold. Hence, we know these benefits are specific to the cold.

It's clear, then, that cold exposure is great for your physical health, but I think there's another important reason why we should do this, and it's a psychological reason. Marcus Aurelius – the Roman emperor and Stoic philosopher, who has been described as the last of the great Roman emperors – wrote a diary to himself that he called his 'meditations', which he never meant to be published. However, one of his generals, who Marcus had asked to destroy the diary, ended up reading it and deciding that it was too important to destroy, and he had it published. In this diary, Marcus reflected that he should engage in regular cold-water bathing and exercise because they both develop character, and it is this character that he would need when facing life's challenges.

Think about that: more than 2000 years ago, a famous Roman emperor was talking about enhancing resilience through exposure to stress. Hormesis in action!

Herein lies the thought experiment: if you can't turn that lovely warm shower to cold for 30 seconds to receive all of these physiological and psychological benefits, then how are you going to deal with really hard shit when it drops in your lap? Because if it hasn't already, it will; and if it has already, it will again – because that's just the way life is.

I interviewed the legendary Professor Mike Tipton on my podcast. Professor Tipton is the world's leading authority on exposure to stresses such as cold water and hypoxia (lack of oxygen at high altitudes). He conducted a case study with a British woman who was cured of her treatment-resistant depression by engaging in regular cold-water swimming, and he says that there are lots of anecdotal reports of people reducing depression and anxiety symptoms through cold-water exposure. Mike thinks that the benefits of cold-water swimming come from a combination of the cold water itself and the social aspect, if you do it with other people. Cold-water swimming is an activity that has exploded in the UK in recent years, with thousands of members participating in different groups.

Other lines of research from combined animal and human studies have demonstrated that regular cold-water exposure has the capacity to:

- decrease inflammation in the body
- positively alter your gut microbiome
- improve metabolic health
- increase brown fat (remember, this is your body's more metabolically active fat)
- improve mood and cognition
- activate anti-oxidant enzymes
- increase mitochondrial biogenesis (new batteries) in your muscle cells.

That's a damned impressive list of benefits just from exposing yourself to cold water on a regular basis. Personally, I started off having cold showers about five years ago and initially had one four times a week, but I found a catch with this: at the start of the week, this little voice would often pop into my head saying, 'It's Monday, you don't have to do one today, because you only need to do four in a week'. It became a willpower fight, so I made a rule: every time I have a shower, I finish it by turning it to cold for 30 seconds. If it's a rule, there's no debate; the willpower fight ended.

I also get into the ocean with a bunch of mates for ten minutes once a week in winter. The water temperature around Melbourne ranges between 11°C and 14°C in winter, which is pretty damned cold. We don't even swim; we just stand around up to our necks in the freezing cold water and laugh at each other, and then go for a coffee or tea and a chat afterwards. I think Mike is right about the social element adding to the benefits.

Mike also gave me some great pointers to share if you are going to go into the ocean in cold temperatures:

- You get all the benefits between 10°C and 15°C – it doesn't need to be any colder.
- He believes that the first few minutes are key due to the cold-water shock response, so you don't need to stay in for long.
- Staying in the water for longer than ten minutes may start to negatively impact some people's immune systems, especially beginners.
- Always go into the water with someone else for safety reasons.
- Do not jump into the water or submerge yourself until you've been in there a few times, because that can cause a gasp reflex, which can cause drowning.
- It's a good idea to talk to your doctor beforehand, especially if you have heart or blood pressure issues or are north of 50 years old.
- Never, ever, do Wim Hof–style breathing (controlled hyperventilation) and swim under the water, because there is a very real risk of passing out and drowning. (This also goes for warm water.) I have actually met someone whose fiancé did this to see how long he could hold his breath under water (this type of breathing increases breath retention), and he passed out and drowned.

Heat stress

Now let's flip things to the other temperature extreme, because it turns out that exposure to uncomfortable levels of heat also confers many metabolic benefits to us humans (as well as a range of other species). The academic research on the metabolic adaptations to heat is largely focused on two main modalities: performing exercise in the heat and engaging in sauna use.

Exercising in the heat has been used for many years by both the military and professional athletes, because it induces a very quick adaptation if they need to go to hot climates to perform. If you live in a hot environment, slowly acclimatising yourself to exercise in the heat can be very beneficial.

That said, most of the research in this area is just concerned with how quickly it can help you to adapt to hot environments, and not on the general health benefits. It turns out that most of the research on the health benefits of heat exposure comes from research on sauna use, but bear in mind that you will be able to get at least some of these benefits from exercising in the heat safely, and maybe even from hot baths – more on this later.

Sauna use, which is referred to as 'sauna bathing,' has been popular in a range of cultures for hundreds of years. It is characterised by short-term exposure to high temperatures. This heat exposure elicits mild hyperthermia and stimulates a wide range of coordinated bodily responses, including cardiovascular, neuroendocrine and cytoprotective mechanisms, positioning sauna bathing as a viable means of extending both lifespan and healthspan.

Sauna basics

Heat and sauna therapy for the purposes of healing, cleansing and purification is an ancient practice that can be found across cultures throughout hundreds – if not thousands – of years. Variations of heat therapy include ancient Roman baths, Native American sweat lodges, Japanese onsen, Russian banyas and Finnish saunas. Modern saunas come in three main varieties – dry, steam and infrared – and all utilise short-term exposure to high temperatures, typically ranging from 45°C to 100°C (113°F to 212°F), depending on the modality chosen.

Dry saunas are based on the traditional Finnish sauna, with low humidity and a high temperature – typically from 80°C to 100°C (176°F to 212°F). Steam saunas have higher humidity, which makes sweating and cooling the body more challenging; therefore, they cannot be as hot as dry saunas, and they are reported to be more uncomfortable and stressful than dry saunas.

Infrared saunas use infrared radiation lamps that emit both visible and infrared light, with the infrared light being either near- or far-infrared spectrums. Far-infrared saunas emit longer wavelengths of infrared light that penetrate tissue to 0.1 millimetres deep, while near-infrared saunas emit shorter wavelengths that can penetrate the body up to 5 millimetres. Some modern infrared saunas are capable of emitting both wavelengths – these are known as 'full spectrum infrared saunas'. Because of the deep tissue penetration, infrared saunas operate at cooler temperatures than dry saunas (typically 45°C to 60°C, or 113°F to 140°F) while still heating up the body.

Physiological and hormonal responses to heat stress

All varieties of sauna heat the body to the point where the usual means of cooling through sweating is not enough to compensate for the extreme heat, so the body elicits a rapid, robust response that primarily affects the skin and cardiovascular systems. The skin heats first, rising to approximately 40°C (104°F). This is followed by changes in core body temperature, rising slowly from 37°C to approximately 38°C (98.6°F to 100.4°F) and then rapidly to approximately 39°C (102.2°F) if exposure lasts long enough. Cardiac output – the volume of blood being pumped out by the heart – may increase by as much as 60 or 70 per cent, so it's easy to see how sauna use mimics some of the benefits of cardiovascular exercise.

Additionally, approximately 50 to 70 per cent of the body's circulation redistributes from the core to the skin to facilitate sweating, driving fluid losses at a rate of approximately 0.6 to 1.0 kilograms per hour. This is why you need to hydrate during and after sauna, and should never mix sauna use with alcohol.

The endocrine (hormonal) system responds to the heat by increasing the production of several important hormones, such as beta-endorphins, which are responsible for the 'pleasure' and 'analgesic' effects of a sauna, and noradrenaline (norepinephrine), which you know by now is associated with improved mood and focused attention. Growth hormone – the secretion of which progressively declines with age and may contribute to obesity, muscle and bone loss, and frailty – increases in a manner that is dependent on time, temperature and frequency of exposure. For example, two 20-minute sauna sessions separated by a 30-minute cooling period have been shown to result in a twofold to fivefold elevation in growth hormone secretion, and sauna use and exercise significantly elevate growth hormone when used together.

Immune system effects

Evidence suggests that certain heat shock proteins (HSPs) play roles in both innate and adaptive immunity, and it has also been suggested that HSPs may offer protection against neurodegenerative diseases. Sauna bathing stimulates the immune system by increasing white-blood-cell, lymphocyte, neutrophil and basophil counts, which may help you to have fewer illnesses – a six-month study reported that participants who engaged in regular sauna baths had significantly fewer colds than the control group over the same time period.

The positive impacts on the immune system are at least partly due to the increase in HSPs – remember, these drive hormesis. In one study, healthy men and women who were exposed to heat for

30 minutes at 73°C (163.4°F) increased HSP72 levels by 49 per cent. In another study, healthy men and women had their HSP70 and HSP90 levels increased by 45 per cent and 38 per cent, respectively, after undergoing deep tissue heat therapy for six days.

Cardiovascular effects

Heat exposure from sauna bathing induces protective mechanisms that promote cardiovascular health, some of which are the same as those experienced during exercise. For example, heart rate has been shown to increase up to 100 beats per minute during moderate-temperature sauna bathing sessions and up to 150 beats per minute during hotter sessions, similar to the increases observed during MVPA.

Heart disease was once contraindicated for saunas, but recent research is proving that saunas can be not only safe but also beneficial for people with cardiovascular disease. A range of findings on cardiovascular health have been reported from the ongoing landmark Kuopio Ischemic Heart Disease (KIHD) Risk Factor Study, which has been following 2315 middle-aged Finnish men for more than 20 years. The study has found that those men who frequented saunas the most (four to seven times per week) had a significantly lower risk of sudden cardiac death, fatal coronary heart disease and fatal cardiovascular disease, compared to those who visited saunas one to three times per week. In addition, the study found that increased sauna use was associated with a 40 per cent reduction in all-cause mortality.

Brain and mental health

Sauna bathing is associated with reduced risk of developing age-related neurodegenerative diseases such as Alzheimer's disease and other forms of dementia in a dose-dependent manner (more frequent bathing has a bigger effect). In the KIHD study mentioned earlier, men who reported using the sauna four to seven times per week had a 66 per cent lower risk of developing dementia and a 65 per cent lower risk of developing Alzheimer's disease, compared to men who reported using the sauna only once weekly. Researchers think there may be multiple mechanisms by which frequent sauna use may protect against these diseases, such as improved blood flow to the brain, improved cardiovascular health and the positive health effects of HSPs.

The health benefits of sauna use also extended to other aspects of mental health. Men participating in the KIHD study who reported using the sauna four to seven times per week had a 77 per cent reduced risk of developing psychotic disorders. Additionally, in a randomised controlled trial of depressed individuals, those who received four weeks of sauna sessions experienced reduced symptoms of depression, and participants in another randomised controlled trial who received a single session of heat therapy experienced an acute antidepressant effect that was apparent within one week of treatment and persisted for six weeks after treatment.

Detoxification

Many websites promote sauna bathing as a way of increasing detoxification, but the evidence for this is not yet as robust as for other health impacts, such as the cardiovascular benefits already mentioned. However, several small studies have demonstrated a benefit. In one study, police officers were treated successfully for methamphetamine exposure using a combination of exercise, nutritional support and sauna therapy, and women with occupational exposure to solvents improved after therapy that included sauna use. Interestingly, the high rate of sweating to assist with cooling the body during sauna bathing has been reported to facilitate higher excretion of some heavy metals, including aluminum (3.75 times higher), cadmium (25 times higher), cobalt (7 times higher) and lead (17 times higher), compared to elimination via urine.

Sauna use to aid in detoxification is a promising additional health benefit, but further research is required to understand the mechanisms.

Other benefits

If all that isn't enough to convince you, a number of studies highlight many other benefits of regular sauna use, including increased cardiac output, endothelial function (how well your veins and arteries function), lower oxidative stress markers and, with infrared sauna use, improved exercise tolerance. Sauna use has also been reported to reduce pain in fibromyalgia patients and fatigue, anxiety and depression in individuals with chronic fatigue syndrome. Sauna use may also help prevent or treat diabetes by improving insulin sensitivity, and improvements in respiratory symptoms have also been reported.

It must be noted, though, that there are several situations in which sauna use is either not recommended or is downright dangerous. For example, sauna use may impact male fertility, at least temporarily: decreases in sperm count, motility and average path velocity following a few weeks of regular sauna use have been reported, although sperm count appears to normalise within a week after cessation of sauna use.

And some warnings: people with hypotension (low blood pressure) should obtain medical advice before using the sauna. People with heat sensitivities (such as those with multiple sclerosis) or unstable angina, people who have recently suffered a heart attack and people who are experiencing an illness accompanied by a fever should avoid the sauna. The sauna should also be avoided if you are drinking alcohol, as most sauna accidents and deaths involve alcohol consumption.

Although it has been recommended in the past that pregnant women avoid saunas, several studies have concluded that sauna use does not disturb the development of the foetus in healthy women, especially if the heat is not extreme.

*

Sauna bathing is clearly associated with many health benefits, from cardiovascular and cognitive health to physical fitness and immune system support. It is generally considered safe for healthy adults and may be safe for special populations with appropriate medical supervision. Heat stress via sauna use upregulates positive molecular mechanisms that protect the body and brain from damage, similar to the responses elicited by MVPA, and may offer a means to slow ageing and extend healthspan.

This is all very well, but what if you don't have a sauna? All is not lost, because it appears that many of the benefits come from the increase in core body temperature and associated increase in HSPs. It has been shown that 20 minutes in a hot tub or hot bath at 40°C is enough to increase core body temperature to the amount required for the release of these magical HSPs. So, grab yourself a good book or switch on a podcast and go for a long, hot soak.

Conclusion

It should be patently clear that exposure to uncomfortable levels of both heat and cold are an absolute must if you want to optimise your physical and mental health and longevity. If you don't live near a cold ocean, regular cold showers will do the trick; if you live in a warm climate all year round, a large plastic tub filled with water and a few bags of ice will work wonders. While regular access to a sauna is optimal, a regular hot bath may well get you many of the same benefits.

Adaptation to heat and cold benefitted many of our ancestors by activating hormetic pathways to make them stronger, and our temperature-controlled, comfortable environments are robbing us of these evolutionarily conserved advantages. We can, however, choose to invoke the spirit of Marcus Aurelius and seek deliberate discomfort to enhance our ability to face life's inevitable challenges.

Or you can choose to stay in your comfort zone. The choice is yours.

Chapter 4

Fuel your ecosystem

'If it came from a plant, eat it. If it was made in a plant, don't.'
– Michael Pollan

The link between diet and health is undeniable, and the good news is that our food choices are, to a large extent, under our control. There are limitations, of course, depending on your personal circumstances, food availability and affordability; but if we are honest, most of us choose what goes into our mouths every day.

However, many of us are confused as to what constitutes a healthy diet, because there's lots of conflicting information out there. The media is somewhat to blame for the confusion by pedalling constant arguments over whether fat, carbohydrate or sugar is the real villain, and there are also some dark forces pulling the strings of the media. In addition, clever food scientists have created a multitude of foods that hijack our brains' reward systems to make us crave more.

Let's start off with some fundamentals. Nutritional science is a very young branch of science. It's only about 300 years old, whereas chemistry, for instance, is about 3000 years old. Secondly, it's really quite difficult and expensive to run good-quality studies. The best form of evidence is a randomised control trial, where you randomly allocate people to either a treatment group or a separate control group (or there may be two different intervention groups). You might have half of the participants randomly assigned to a low-fat diet and the other half to a low-carbohydrate diet to see which group loses the most weight, or controls their diabetes better. An even more robust study might then do a crossover design, where the people on the low-fat diet switch to the low-carbohydrate diet after 12 weeks, and vice versa.

To make it more robust again, you also have to control for other factors, such as how much study participants are exercising, how much they're sleeping and how much stress is in their lives – these are called 'confounding variables'. The best thing to do is have participants live in a controlled environment (such as a metabolic ward) where you can measure exactly what they eat, how much they move and how much they sleep. But who the hell wants to live on a metabolic ward for 24 weeks?

When this does happen, it's often students who are paid to do it. Do their results translate directly to older people? Probably not.

So, given all of these difficulties, nutritional scientists have historically relied on observational studies: they take a bunch of people (called a 'cohort') and follow them for maybe 5, 10 or 20 years, and perform nutritional surveys on them maybe every six months at best. These are called 'food frequency questionnaires', which are really quite a poor way to get an accurate picture of participants' overall diet because people forget what they eat, tend to under-report unhealthy foods and sometimes just lie.

The researchers follow the cohort and see, for example, who gets heart disease or diabetes and who doesn't. Then they look back at the data to see what differences (if any) there were in what they ate, and they'll try to infer conclusions around that. They have often then made public health recommendations based on these observations.

In all other branches of science, observational studies are used to generate hypothesis, and that's it! That's what they should do. But in nutrition, we have actually created dietary guidelines based off these really weak observational studies. Some of the early studies that drew conclusions about the impact of diet on heart disease didn't account for whether or not participants smoked or how much exercise they did, which is just plain crazy.

The first recommendation to lower cholesterol in the diet came from the USA in 1977, and in 1983 they went a step further and told people that they should be eating a low-fat diet, and particularly one low in saturated fats. These recommendations were picked up by other nations, and hundreds of millions of people were told that they should eat less fat and more carbohydrate.

This unintentionally spawned the production of a variety of cheap, carbohydrate-based foods that were highly palatable and profitable, and over time these foods have been increasingly infiltrated by different types of sugar, the worst of which are fructose and high-fructose corn syrup. Both of these stimulate the liver to create harmful small dense LDL particles (the really bad 'cholesterol'), increase liver fat (thereby causing fatty liver disease), decrease insulin sensitivity, increase blood pressure through formation of uric acid, increase trigylcerides, promote weight gain and obesity, and damage mitochondria in liver cells.

In addition, these foods were accompanied by the production and sale of enormous amounts of refined seed oils, which were marketed as healthy because they reduced cholesterol. These seed oils include cottonseed, canola, sunflower, grapeseed, safflower and rice bran oils, and they have been accompanied by big increases in peanut and soybean oils, which are legume oils.

These oils are able to reduce cholesterol (although the clinical impact of that is highly debatable), but we now know that when these oils are heated – as in cooking – they produce a range of highly toxic, carcinogenic substances called 'aldehydes'; they oxidise the fats in our body (which is very bad); they cause systemic inflammation; and they are linked to a range of poor health outcomes.

Check out figure 4.1, which shows how US consumption of sugar and seed oils has increased at an alarming rate during the comfort revolution. Consumption of sugar per person has increased from around three teaspoons a day in the early 1800s to between 35 and 40 teaspoons today – a tenfold increase! For good health, we need around 1.5 to 3 grams of omega-6 polyunsaturated fat, but we are now consuming between 26 and 40 grams per day, largely from refined seed oils in fast food and processed foods.

Figure 4.1: US consumption of sugar and polyunsaturated fat

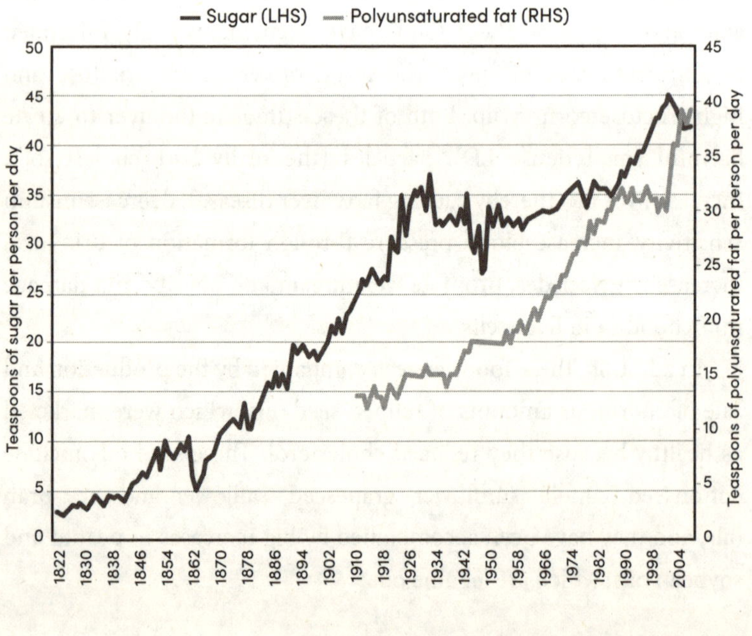

We now know the randomised controlled trial evidence available in 1977 and 1983 did not support those low-fat recommendations, and because of them, we're eating a diet that is very high in ultra-processed foods and drinks (UPFs).

The problem with ultra-processed foods

What do we mean by ultra-processed foods? First let me give you the academic definition, and then I'll discuss what this means in the real world.

The term was coined by researchers from Brazil and is the basis of what is called the 'NOVA classification' of foods. This essentially classifies foods into four categories based on the level of processing:

1. Unprocessed or minimally processed foods
2. Processed culinary ingredients
3. Processed foods
4. Ultra-processed foods.

Let's look at the application of the NOVA classification to an orange. An orange is a category-one food, but commercial processing can turn it into a category-three or category-four food.

To make it a processed, category-three food, a commercial processor would peel the whole oranges, slice them up, remove the excess juice and then put the oranges in an oven or a dehydrator to preserve them for later consumption, and maybe sell them as dried orange slices.

To make it a UPF (a category-four food), the whole oranges would be washed and then squeezed by a machine, with the pulp, oils and oxygen removed. Why remove the oxygen? Because it extends the shelf life. The juice is then heated or pasteurised so that it inactivates enzymes and kills potentially harmful microbes. Then they add artificial food additives, including preservatives, colours and often sweeteners.

This is exactly the orange juice that you buy in a supermarket. This processing means that it can be kept in large tanks for up to a year before being packaged and sent off to supermarkets. So, it can be a year and a half or more from the picking of the real orange to the point where it actually passes your lips. There's also the issue of the huge amount of fructose delivered very quickly to your liver and other organs that drives weight gain and inflammation, but more on that later.

The older dietary guidelines focused a fair bit on fat, carbohydrates and protein, and there were lots of issues with this, including the unhelpful and incorrect demonising of fat that led to the production of many carbohydrate-rich UPFs in the first place. Instead of focusing on these macronutrients, the NOVA classification takes into consideration all physical, chemical and biological methods used during the food productive process, which I think is a much better system. It doesn't mean that the nutrient content of foods is unimportant, but we need to understand how to put foods together to meet our nutritional needs. The NOVA classification helps to guide the big picture, pushing us towards eating more whole foods.

Importantly, the NOVA classification also recognises that some processing is OK and even beneficial. Take cooking – this is a form of food processing, and developing this skill was critical for the development of our species, because it helps us make food safer and tastier, and it releases many nutrients, making it easier for us to meet our nutritional needs.

It is the UPFs that are the big problem. These category-four foods are made from already highly processed ingredients and contain very few (if any) category-one, whole foods.

The ingredients list of a UPF may sound as if it belongs in the pharmacy rather than the kitchen. These ingredients include highly processed sugar, protein and oil derivatives such as high-fructose corn syrup, maltodextrin, protein isolates and hydrogenated oil. There may also be additives to improve the food's shelf life, texture, flavour and so on, such as emulsifiers, thickeners, colours, flavours, flavour enhancers and artificial sweeteners.

It's actually all brilliant science, because these additives make the final products longer-lasting and more palatable, and encourage us to over-consume them. Unfortunately, the clever food scientists who create these foods in the lab don't have our health in mind, but rather food industry profits. Food is a competitive market, and their goal is to tap into the reward centres of our brains to drive as much consumption of their product as possible.

You probably won't be surprised to hear that the UPF category contains items such as sugar-sweetened or artificially sweetened beverages, confectionary, ice-cream, most commercial chocolates (although a little proper dark chocolate made with real cocoa can be good), packaged savoury snacks, burgers, pies, chicken nuggets and other processed meat, frozen dishes, pizza and all fast foods. However, it also includes breakfast cereals and breads, which are everyday foods for many people.

Although some cereal manufacturers have yielded to pressure in recent years and reduced the amount of sugar and salt in their products while increasing the content of whole grains, most breakfast cereals are highly processed crap with way too much sugar and refined starch, and little fibre, and contain colourings and other nasty additives. Avoid these like the plague. Your best bet, and a terrific whole food, is good old-fashioned rolled oats. Not the instant type, though – I'm talking about the proper stuff. It takes only a few minutes to whip them up into a porridge or soak them overnight for a bircher-style muesli, or have them with unsweetened full-fat yoghurt, berries, nuts and seeds. That is a natural, nutritionally dense breakfast. Breakfast cereal isn't.

Bread is another food that many people are surprised is on the list. Although it has become a cornerstone of many diets, most breads are firmly in the UPF basket. Artisan breads, such as sourdough bread made by your local bakery (especially wholegrain or rye), are a notable exception – these are classified as category-three processed foods, and a certain amount of this in your diet is fine. They are made using generations-old techniques, and in the case of sourdough, the fermentation acts as a natural preservative to extend the shelf life in a healthy way.

Compare that to a mass-produced supermarket loaf, which contains a particularly nasty preservative called 'proprionate', often labelled as 'calcium salt' (and sometimes not even appearing on the ingredients list, even though it's in there). Proprionate has been shown to impair insulin action in both mice and humans, making supermarket breads a significant contributor to the diabetes epidemic. It makes me laugh – or rather, cry! – when so-called diabetes educators tell diabetic patients to switch to supermarket wholemeal breads. As well as containing proprionate, two slices of wholemeal bread will raise your blood sugar as much as a Snickers bar!

Here's a little test to try at home that I learnt from my colleague Dr Joanna McMillan. Place a piece of supermarket white bread on the roof of your mouth and don't chew it. That fluffy white crap will literally start to dissolve as the enzymes in your saliva easily access the starch and break it down. In contrast, wholegrain sourdough bread will still be there hours later! You need to chew it – your body has to work hard to break it all down, releasing the energy and nutrients way down in the small intestine. That's the way digestion is supposed to work.

When thinking about your own consumption of UPFs, beware of the so-called healthy foods such as muesli bars, meat substitutes such as soy burgers, and many ready-to-eat meals. Beware, too, of the latest trend of 'health halo' plant-based foods – many are in fact just more UPFs. I'm all for you eating a bean burger made with legumes and veggies if you're a vegetarian or vegan, but a burger made with soy protein isolate, emulsifiers, flours and other additives is just more ultra-processed crap.

These UPFs are destroying both our physical health and mental fitness. My definition? Shit food! And we eat it by the truckload.

These hyperpalatable foods bring you short-term pleasure and comfort when you are stressed or anxious, but ultimately they wreck your physical health over time and erode your mental fitness. Clever food scientists know that combinations of fat, salt and sugar are 'the neurobiology of preference', a geeky science term that means that our brains are hard-wired to prefer them. Sugar is a readily available energy source, fat is energy dense, and salt is necessary for survival, which is why our ancestors' brains were wired to release a hit of dopamine when they ate them, which told them, 'That tasted good, eat some more'. (Dopamine is the neurotransmitter that stimulates motivation and goal-directed behaviour.) Combining them and adding in some emulsifiers to enhance the texture and flavour gives the brain a 'nuclear reward' that it was not conditioned to deal with, which is why we reach for more.

These UPFs are becoming dominant in the global food supply, with developed nations consuming up 50 per cent or more of their total calories as UPF, and middle-income countries consuming around 30 per cent and increasing. And it's killing us. Death by comfort and pleasure!

They are displacing more nutritious foods, but they can also have an impact in moderate amounts. In Australia, the 'SMILES trial' found that even in those participants who ate healthily most of the time, eating UPFs such as fast food on a semi-regular basis resulted in an increase in depressive symptoms.

In addition, a French study followed 26,730 individuals without depressive symptoms at baseline for an average of 5.4 years. Results showed that those in the highest quartile (25 per cent) of UPF intake had a 31 per cent increased risk of developing depression compared to those in the lowest quartile, and a 10 per cent increase in UPF consumption was associated with a 21 per cent increased risk of depression.

In Spain, 14,907 university graduates who were free of depression at the start of the study were followed for around 10.3 years. In a strikingly similar result to the French study, participants in the highest quartile intake of UPF intake had a 33 per cent higher risk of developing depression than participants in the lowest quartile.

Many other studies have shown similarly detrimental effects on other diseases and conditions. A UK study showed that a 10 per cent increase in the amount of UPF in the diet translated to an 18 per cent increase in obesity prevalence in men and 17 per cent in women. Two French studies of over 100,000 people found that increasing UPF in your diet by 10 per cent was associated with a significant increase of more than 10 per cent in the risk of overall cancer and in the risk of cardiovascular disease. Those with the highest intakes increased their risks by a whopping 25 per cent.

A recent review of 43 studies found that dietary UPF exposure was associated with being overweight or obese, the development of cardiometabolic risk factors, cancer, type 2 diabetes, cardiovascular diseases, irritable bowel syndrome, depression, frailty conditions and all-cause mortality! One recent study found that regularly consuming more than four serves a day of UPF increases your risk of death by any cause by a whopping 62 per cent compared to those who ate the least! Every extra serving increased the risk of death by any cause by 18 per cent.

From a scientific point of view, observational studies don't give us very strong evidence. However, the plethora of studies from around the world that I've just mentioned show the dangers of UPFs with great consistency, so the evidence becomes stronger. When you add in the existence of plausible biological mechanisms to drive these disease processes, such as the proprionate studies and other studies on the harmful effects of food colourings and emulsifiers, the evidence becomes very clear.

Randomised controlled trials offer us the strongest evidence, but they are pretty rare in the world of nutritional research because, as I explained earlier, they are very expensive and difficult to do. In my opinion, one randomised control trial on the impact of UPF puts the evidence of harm from these foods beyond any reasonable doubt. This was a beautifully designed study in which subjects went through a crossover design of two different diets: one was a healthy diet and the other was a diet of UPF that was matched with the healthy diet in terms of calories, fat, carbohydrates and protein. Each group stayed on that diet for 14 days, and then they switched over to the other diet for the same time. In terms of study design, it doesn't get any better than that.

The researchers told the subjects to eat as much as they needed until they felt sated. The researchers discovered that when both groups were eating the UPF diet, they consumed about 500 calories extra a day, mostly in the form of processed carbohydrate (the highly palatable foods). We know from other studies that processed carbohydrate impacts negatively on our hormones, particularly our insulin and other hunger hormones. So, it's not just about the calories in the food – it's what they do to your hormones that actually drives you to eat more food.

Interestingly, the UPF in this diet wasn't as bad as you might think. It wasn't full of chips, lollies, pizzas and sweetened drinks, but rather mostly inconspicuous foods such as mass-produced packaged foods, breads, breakfast cereals and frozen meals.

These, I think you'll agree, are very alarming facts. Making matters worse is the situation summarised by the title of one of the most concerning research papers that I have ever read: 'Ultra-processed products are becoming dominant in the global food system'. This paper was published in 2013, and UPF production and consumption has been spreading like wildfire since then.

Big supermarkets also play a role in this food fiasco. These UPFs are very cheap to make and highly profitable for the manufacturers and supermarkets alike, so they get prominent shelf space, encouraging us to buy more. We are also doing more and more of our shopping at these big supermarkets, which helps to drive sales of UPF. Here's a tip for you: do the vast majority of your supermarket shopping around the outside, because that is where the real food tends to be – the crap tends to be located in the inner aisles.

There have been a number of research studies from around the world looking at the amount of processed food in the diet of different countries over the last couple of decades. Here's what they've found:

- Of the countries studied, Malaysia and Spain came in at the lowest rates, with 23 and 24 per cent (respectively) of calories consumed coming from UPF.
- France comes in between 30 per cent and 36 per cent.
- Data from Australia in 2008 showed that about 42 per cent of all calories consumed were from UPF, and it's been on the rise since then.
- In Canada, UPF comprised 45.7 per cent of calories in 2015, and for children it was over 50 per cent.

- In the UK, UPF consumption between 2008 and 2016 was 54.3 per cent of all calories consumed.
- In the USA, it was 57.9 per cent of all calories eaten in 2010.
- A more recent US study reported that kids between the ages of 2 and 19 years now get a whopping 67 per cent of all calories from UPF. Two-thirds of all calories!
- Overall, sales of UPF are highest in Australasia, North America, Europe and Latin America, but are growing rapidly in Asia, the Middle East and Africa.

Big Food and nutritional disinformation

You'd think that, given all of this information, organisations such as The Heart Foundation and dietitian bodies such as the Dietitians Association of Australia, who help advise the population on healthy diets, would be expending huge amounts of effort telling us not to eat those foods, including breakfast cereals and commercial breads.

Not so. And I think it's a disgrace.

A few years back, Australian investigative journalist Maryanne Demasi uncovered why this may be. She spent a year investigating the undue influence that sugar and breakfast cereal lobbies have over Diabetes Australia and the Dietitians Association of Australia, the primary body for public nutrition advice. Demasi exposed the concerning relationship between these bodies and the Australian Breakfast Cereal Manufacturers Forum (ABCMF), whose members include companies such as Freedom Foods, Kellogg's Australia, Nestlé and Sanitarium.

In particular she highlighted that, in 2017, the Federal Assistant Minister for Rural Health, David Gillespie, released a statement encouraging people to eat more 'grain fibre' to reduce their risk of type 2 diabetes and heart disease, claiming a new study showed it could 'save the economy almost $3.3 billion in healthcare and lost productivity costs'. It turns out that this study was commissioned and entirely funded by Kellogg's Australia, a breakfast cereal manufacturer that stood to profit from the promotion of 'grain fibre'. The 70-page report relied on a mere five studies (which is pretty ridiculous to start with), and to quote Brisbane-based nutritionist Anthony Power, 'Two have Kellogg's funding, one has weak methodology and in fact one study clearly states the evidence is "too weak" to support a link between fibre intake and reducing risk of diabetes, yet they cite it as support for their argument'.

Medical research reviewer Cochrane conducts gold-standard systematic reviews, and had previously concluded in two separate reviews that there was not enough evidence to suggest that whole-grain foods had a preventative effect on either type 2 diabetes or cardiovascular risk factors. Demasi pointed out that this seems to have been ignored by the Dietitians Association of Australia and its spokespeople, who often target ads to the public promoting its sponsor's (ABCMF's) products.

In a campaign hilariously named 'Wheatileaks', Demasi also reported on leaked documents that revealed the secret tactics used by ABCMF to sanitise negative messages about breakfast cereals. The confidential documents revealed the organisation's strategy for influencing public opinion about the benefits of cereal products by paying a range of high-profile dietitians who they called 'key media influencers' for 'neutralising negative coverage on breakfast cereals by actively engaging with the media'.

Essentially, its strategy was to pay influential health professionals to peddle its own industry-funded science.

Demasi reported that ACBMF paid the Dietitians Association of Australia $23,000 per year and provided materials to them to be used on their website. They also had an 'active defence' strategy against those who were a threat to their messaging. These included authors of anti-sugar books Sarah Wilson and David Gillespie (not the same David Gillespie I just mentioned), as well as University of Sydney obesity researcher Dr Kieron Rooney and Dr Gary Fettke, an orthopaedic surgeon who was sanctioned by the Medical Board of Australia for prescribing low-sugar diets to patients with type 2 diabetes. He eventually received an apology from the Medical Board of Australia after the publication of the 'Wheatileaks' story. The Dietitians Association of Australia also announced that it would be ceasing its corporate relationships with food manufacturing and food industry associations by 31 December 2018, which it did. Bravo Maryanne Demasi!

All of this is just the tip of the iceberg, because it turns out that Big Food is even more powerful than Big Tobacco and uses many of the same tactics. That's partly because tobacco companies such as Philip Morris International started to 'diversify' into the expanding food and beverage sector in the 1980s, purchasing companies in this sector and then transferring employees, technology and business practices from the dwindling tobacco sector. These business practices include sponsorship of influential bodies linked to the sector and direction of research designed to minimise the messages of harm about their unhealthy products.

Philip Morris International bought both General Foods Corporation and Kraft Foods Inc in the 1980s and combined them under the name of 'Kraft Foods' in 1990. In 2015, it merged with Heinz to create Kraft Heinz, which now has eight billion-dollar brands and global sales of over US$26 billion in 2021. It is the fifth biggest food and beverage company in the world and one of the biggest global producers of UPFs. Other big players include Nestlé (the world's biggest food company, with around $90 billion in annual sales), Mondelēz, PepsiCo, The Coca-Cola Company, McDonald's and other fast-food chains.

They, and other industry partners, fund research that favours industry and criticises evidence that is counter to their interests to create public uncertainty. An example is the industry-funded research organisation the International Life Sciences Institute (ILSI), a shadowy institution that was founded by a Coca-Cola executive and is almost entirely funded by industry. It positions itself as 'a global, nonprofit federation committed to improving public and planetary health worldwide by convening representatives from the academic, public and private sectors to advance evidence-based scientific research'. Sounds impressive; however, according to *The New York Times*, it championed the interests of the tobacco industry in the 1980s and recently successfully lobbied the Chinese government to reframe its obesity policy to focus on physical activity instead of diet. In 2020, the Alliance Against Conflict of Interest (AACI) described ILSI as 'a lobbying arm of the food industry' and said it was notorious for pursuing policy influence globally, especially with respect to sugary foods and beverages. They accused ILSI of influencing the WHO's and governments' decisions in their favour. Dodgy stuff indeed!

In Indonesia, Mondelēz, Nestlé and Coca-Cola have all engaged in significant corporate social responsibility projects to strengthen their relationships with local NGOs, religious institutions and the government. Similarly, in South Africa, Nestlé partnered with the National Department of Basic Education to provide 'nutritional education' (and peddle its products) to over half of all South African primary school students. Additionally, according to the Industry Documents Library, Russian hackers published emails showing that, in 2014, Coca-Cola donated over $1.5 million to the non-profit Global Energy Balance Network to promote the idea that exercise played a greater role in public health than what the public ate or drank.

As we've seen earlier, these UPFs are strongly linked to a range of chronic diseases, but they are hyperpalatable and potentially addictive.

It's clear that government guidelines around food are influenced by the big producers of these foods, and until governments and other health bodies rid themselves of this influence and follow the lead of Brazil and other Latin American countries in strongly advising people to avoid UPFs, I suggest that you ignore their advice.

My three simple food rules

So, what can you do? I have three simple food rules to get you out of nutritional comfort and convenience while enhancing both your physical and mental health:

1. Eat a low HI diet.
2. Feed both your brains.
3. Embrace nutritional hormesis.

Rule 1: eat a low HI diet

This is the only diet you'll ever need, and it's very simple to follow. You've probably heard of the glycemic index (GI), which can be useful for choosing carbohydrate-rich foods, but it's not the be-all and end-all of how we should eat. I believe it's much more important to eat a low HI (human interference) diet.

Basically, this means eating a diet that is rich in real foods and minimally processed foods, and avoiding UPFs as much as possible. How do you know if it's real food? It's very simple: real foods don't have ingredients; real foods *are* ingredients!

If you can see that a piece of food has been alive recently and minimally interfered with by humans, then eat it. It's probably fine. If it's grown in the ground or on a tree or vine, or until recently was running around on four legs or swimming, then it's generally

OK to eat. However, if you're looking at a Krispy Kreme donut, for example, and you're saying to yourself, 'I don't remember seeing you running around on four legs,' then it doesn't pass the low HI test.

That doesn't mean you can never eat it, though. I like to combine the low HI rule with the 80/20 rule, where roughly 80 per cent of the stuff that you eat should be low HI and the other 20 per cent is your treat foods (or 'discretionary foods'). If you go by that rule, you will dramatically decrease your risk of many diseases and all-cause mortality. I think we're going to see stronger and stronger evidence come out about the dangers of these UPFs for both us and our kids.

If you are somebody who eats meat, think about a piece of fresh fish versus fish fingers, or a piece of steak versus sausages or a pie. If you're vegetarian or vegan, think about lentils versus soy burgers. Low HI doesn't just mean foods that have not been interfered with at all, because humans have been interfering with food for most of our existence. Cooking is a form of interference, as is preserving foods. However, there's a big difference between fermenting, smoking or salting foods to preserve them and the wide range of preservatives used in industrial food processing, such as sodium nitrate in meats, butylated hydroxyanisole (BHA) in cereals, chips, candy and food packaging, trans fats, high-fructose corn syrup (in ludicrous amounts of food) and the insulin-disrupting proprionate that's added to baked goods.

As well as eating a range of very low HI foods – such as fruit, vegetables, tubers, and fresh fish and meat – we can also make better choices when it comes to processed foods, such as choosing:

- extra-virgin olive oil instead of seed oils
- butter instead of margarine
- artisan bread instead of supermarket bread
- cocoa-rich dark chocolate instead of milk chocolate
- rolled oats instead of processed breakfast cereals.

Eating a low HI diet that follows the 80/20 rule ensures two things: that you minimise the amount of nasty shit that gets into your body from UPFs, and that you get lots of vitamins, minerals and biologically active phytochemicals to move you towards optimal health.

Take breakfast as an example. Manufacturers prominently list nutrients on the packaging – 'high in calcium' or 'high in iron', for example. However, if you eat a commercial breakfast cereal (as many people do), you get maybe 10 or 15 nutrients – which are often chemical derivatives of real nutrients, because the food processing destroys many natural nutrients – along with a heap of nasty colours, flavours, preservatives and, often, a significant amount of sugar. If you replaced that cereal with rolled oats, unsweetened Greek yoghurt (and maybe a little kefir), berries, nuts and seeds – or an omelette with a handful of veggies – you'd literally be getting thousands of nutrients. What most people don't realise is that fruit and vegetables contain thousands of biologically active phytochemicals that are likely to interact in a number of ways to prevent disease and promote health.

With your 20 per cent treat foods, choose wisely. If you like chocolate or ice-cream, buy the best damned chocolate or ice-cream that you can afford and savour it. Remember that your 20 per cent also includes what you drink, so if you like alcohol, that's included. For me, being Irish and ex-military, it's an easy choice between alcohol and breakfast cereal! Think about the stuff that is sacrosanct for you in terms of pleasurable food and drink, and have your 20 per cent guilt free. If you need to shift your health, maybe go 90/10, rather than 80/20. I don't recommend going 100/0, as it's really not sustainable (and it's also a fair bit obsessive). Orthorexia nervosa is a relatively new condition that is identified by obsessive healthy eating and exercise, and it can be very bad for your wellbeing. You should get some pleasure from food, but your diet is primarily about nourishing your body and brain.

Rule 2: feed both your brains

At one level, all you are is an ecosystem of trillions of cells, and most of these cells contain your DNA. You have a grand total of 20,000 or so genes in your DNA, but millions of bacteria live inside you. What we now know is that you're not just an ecosystem of cells; you're a super-ecosystem, and we know that your gut bacteria play a really essential role in both your physical and mental health. Furthermore, the science is now very clear that the composition of your gut bacteria is heavily influenced by your diet. It's also influenced by whether you were delivered via a natural birth or a caesarean section, whether you were breastfed or bottle-fed, whether you were allowed to play in the dirt, whether or not you had a pet, and the amount of antibiotics you've had, but you can't control those things now.

What you can control is the composition of our diet. We know that there is a two-way interaction between your brain and your gut, which are connected through the vagus nerve. You may be surprised to know that the vast majority of your serotonin, which is an important neurotransmitter for mood and sleep, is actually produced in your gut, not in your brain.

Your gut bacteria have a lot to do with the production of serotonin, and influence your mood. Research has also shown that people who are obese have a different balance of bacteroides and firmicutes (two types of gut bacteria) than people who are lean.

However, your brain influences your gut bacteria – if you are chronically stressed, it can negatively change the composition of your gut bacteria. Good stress management strategies are useful, then, but your diet has a much bigger impact on your gut bacteria. Certain foods are really beneficial for our gut bacteria, and certain other foods – you'll not be surprised to hear that UPFs are among them – are bad for the composition of our gut bacteria and crowd out our good bacteria.

It's been suggested that you can improve the composition of your gut bugs by eating fewer processed carbohydrates and sugars and more 'resistant starch', or microbiota-accessible carbohydrates (which is a bit of a mouthful but basically means the elements of certain carbohydrate-rich foods that feed your good bugs). Resistant starch is found in good amounts in such foods as peas, beans, lentils, certain fruits and vegetables, and natural whole grains (not breakfast cereals, but oats, barley, couscous, quinoa, rye and other unprocessed whole grains).

A recent study conducted by scientists at Stanford University showed that fermented foods should also be right at the top of your list, and that if you're transitioning from a poor diet, focusing on bringing fermented foods into your diet before you up your intake of resistant starch (fibre), is the way to go for most people. You do need to build up a tolerance to these foods, though, as diving straight in with lots of them can give you a stomach-ache. Try introducing a little unsweetened kefir (a fermented milk drink), some sauerkraut, kimchi, kombucha, miso soup, apple cider vinegar and pickles, as well as live yoghurts and fermented cheeses.

Another hugely important factor in creating a healthy microbiome is eating a wide variety of food, especially fruit, vegetables and legumes. It's been shown that the Hadza (the hunter-gatherer tribe from East Africa I discussed earlier) have a much greater diversity of bacteria in their microbiome than people from Western countries because they eat a much greater range of natural foods. At the end of this chapter, you'll find a link to a 40-foods-per-week challenge worksheet, where you try to eat 40 different foods (including at least 30 from plants) of a range of different colours. Once you've mastered that, there's also a 50-foods challenge.

So, remember: you're not just one ecosystem; you're a super-ecosystem, and you've got to feed your good bugs.

Rule 3: embrace nutritional hormesis

By now you know that hormesis is the process of exposing yourself to small-to-moderate amounts of stress in order to drive stress resistance or resilience. It turns out that hormesis applies to food as well through two well-established processes: intermittent fasting and hormetic phytochemicals. Let's explore the mechanism behind each of these and some recommendations for implementing them.

Intermittent periods of fasting drive two processes that are evolutionarily conserved (meaning they have occurred in a range of species unchanged across evolutionary timelines):

1. They increase multiple forms of stress resistance.
2. They produce a rapid onset of beneficial effects.

There are three common, evidence-based ways to perform intermittent fasting, and they have overlapping themes and benefits.

The first is to extend your overnight fast. It's wise to do this gradually so your body has time to adjust. It would appear from the available evidence to date that the best method is to finish eating and drinking at around 7 p.m. and then only have water until the next day. Start with a 12-hour window and then gradually increase the duration of the fast up to around 16 hours, with an 8-hour feeding window. This is called the '16:8 protocol', and many researchers refer to this as 'time-restricted eating'. The idea is to do this several days a week. I personally like this protocol, but I don't do it seven days a week because I like to drink alcohol some evenings. I often don't get to 16 hours, and that's OK, because anything over 12 is beneficial. Fasting for more than 12 hours acts as a metabolic trigger to switch liver metabolism from using glucose as a fuel source to breaking down fatty acids into ketones, which serve as energy for our cells but also act as cellular signalling molecules. These metabolic changes increase mitochondrial numbers (the batteries in your cells), drive the creation of new blood vessels, increase exercise capacity and enhance longevity.

The second way has been popularised by TV host Michael Mosely (although he didn't invent it) and is called the '5:2 diet'. This is where you eat normally for five days and then drastically reduce your calorie intake to between 500 and 800 on the other two days of the week. Many people find this to be a great way to achieve weight loss, but it appears to benefit men more than women (although some women do very well on it). If you are after more rapid weight loss, or if you need to lose a lot of weight, variations on this theme include alternate-day fasting – where you eat normally one day and then dramatically reduce your calories the next day (or even fast completely on alternate days) – until you reach your goal weight.

The third method is more drastic, but the idea is to only do it occasionally – between one and four times a year – to give yourself a cellular spring-clean: a four- or five-day (although some people go for longer) water-only fast. This induces a process called 'autophagy', where the body cleans out senescent (zombie-like) cells, which are much more prone to turn cancerous, so this type of fasting can reduce your cancer risk as well as having many other benefits. (There may not be much point in this if you're under 40, though, as the process of autophagy is probably still working well for you – like many bodily processes, it becomes less effective as we age.) Some people will tell you that fasting for four or five days is dangerous, but unless you have a health condition such as type 1 diabetes, that's not the case. The documented world record fast was undertaken by a very overweight (200-kilogram) Scottish man in the early 1970s, who asked his doctor to supervise him while he fasted to lose weight, and he ended up fasting for 382 days! Yep, you read that right. He lost 120 kilograms and managed to keep it off, and his story was published in a medical journal in 1973.

Multiple studies confirm the beneficial effects of short-term fasting in improving cellular health, reducing inflammation, protecting against radiation, and reducing your risk of metabolic disorders, certain cancers and even infections such as cerebral malaria.

The studies on the different types of intermittent fasting are way too numerous to go through in detail, but here are some of the benefits that have been discovered:

- *Weight loss:* Weight loss, especially loss of visceral fat (the dangerous fat underneath your stomach muscles), is a very common reason to engage in the different types of intermittent fasting, and the benefits come from the combination of a couple of different mechanisms. First, by compressing your eating window, or having days of full or partial fast, you reduce the calories that you consume. In addition, intermittent fasting can also change the function of certain hormones to facilitate weight loss. Lower insulin levels help with weight loss, and fasting can also result in higher human growth hormone levels and increased amounts of noradrenaline (norepinephrine), which increase the breakdown of body fat for energy. Short-term fasting may, therefore, actually increase your metabolic rate, helping you burn even more calories. It's important to note, though, that not everyone experiences the same weight loss, and different types of fasting can have different impacts, so the key is to run experiments.
- *Brain benefits:* Intermittent fasting improves various metabolic features known to be important for brain health. It also helps reduce oxidative stress, inflammation, blood sugar levels and insulin resistance. Fasting also increases levels of the brain hormone BDNF, the deficiency of which has been implicated in depression and various other brain problems. In addition, animal

studies have shown that intermittent fasting may increase the growth of new nerve cells (which should have benefits for brain function), protect against brain damage from strokes, delay the onset of Alzheimer's disease or reduce its severity, and protect against such other neurodegenerative diseases as Parkinson's disease and Huntington's disease; however, more research in humans is needed.

- *Heart benefits:* Heart disease is currently the world's biggest killer, and a number of well-known risk factors for developing heart disease have been shown to be improved by various forms of intermittent fasting, such as blood pressure, blood triglycerides, total cholesterol and the 'bad' LDL cholesterol (especially small dense LDL), blood sugar levels and inflammatory markers. Most of this research comes from animal studies, but there are also compelling data from human studies, including a 2020 study on patients with metabolic syndrome who compressed their eating window to 10 hours a day for 12 weeks and experienced reductions in weight, waist circumference, blood pressure, LDL cholesterol and blood sugars, as well as improvements in sleep.
- *Reduced risk of certain types of cancer (and improved treatment outcomes):* Cancer is characterised by uncontrolled growth of cells. Fasting has been shown to have several beneficial effects on metabolism that may lead to reduced risk of cancer. There's also some evidence that fasting reduces various side effects of chemotherapy in humans.
- *Reduced risk of metabolic diseases:* Type 2 diabetes has become a very common diagnosis in recent decades. Its main feature is high blood sugar levels in the context of insulin resistance; therefore, anything that reduces insulin resistance should help lower blood sugar levels and protect against type 2 diabetes. Interestingly, intermittent fasting has been shown to have major

benefits for insulin resistance, and to lead to an impressive reduction in blood sugar levels. However, there may be some differences between the sexes: one 2005 study showed that blood sugar management in women actually worsened after a 22-day intermittent fasting protocol.

- *Cellular repair:* As mentioned previously, when you fast, the cells in your body initiate a cellular 'waste removal' process called 'autophagy'. This involves the cells breaking down and metabolising broken and dysfunctional proteins that build up inside cells over time. Increased autophagy may provide protection against several diseases, including cancer and neurodegenerative diseases such as Alzheimer's disease.
- *Possible lifespan increase:* Many studies performed on worms, fruit flies, rodents and non-human primates have shown that both long-term calorie restriction and intermittent fasting extend lifespan. These animals are much easier to study than humans, and although it's always risky to extend the findings of animal studies to humans, the known benefits for metabolism and all sorts of health markers – such as inflammation, oxidative stress, blood pressure, blood glucose, insulin and blood lipids – make it quite likely that intermittent fasting could help you to live longer if it becomes a long-term habit. That said, the type and frequency of fasting required to best extend human lifespan is far from being determined. Intermittent fasting, though, has become very popular in the anti-ageing movement, which boasts many eminent scientists. If I were a betting man, I'd bet on intermittent fasting increasing lifespan.

So, the benefits of intermittent fasting are clear, but what about hormetic phytochemicals? Over a decade ago, I read the landmark scientific study in this area, which was published by scientists at the

National Institute on Aging in the USA, called 'Hormetic dietary phytochemicals'. It discussed compelling evidence from epidemiological studies suggesting that certain dietary phytochemicals that are found in a range of plants could protect against chronic disorders such as cancer, inflammatory diseases and cardiovascular diseases. The reason they are protective is because they are actually toxins – but rather than being harmful to us, they have a net benefit because they activate cellular stress response pathways, upregulating our protection against disease by switching on protective genes.

In the words of the philosopher Fredrich Nietzsche, 'What does not kill me makes me stronger'.

The researchers also reported on emerging evidence that several dietary phytochemicals also benefit the nervous system and, when consumed regularly, may reduce the risk of brain disorders such as Alzheimer's disease and Parkinson's disease. Additionally, many of them have epigenetic effects, meaning that they are able to regulate the expression of our genes to improve our health.

It's thought that these chemicals are produced by the plants due to their need to protect themselves against attacks from bacteria, fungi, viruses and hazardous environmental changes, and the plants tend to concentrate these defensive chemicals in their most vulnerable parts: their leaves, flowers and roots. Like moderate exercise, and cold and heat exposure, many of these 'poisons' also have classic hormetic properties for humans, being harmful at high doses but beneficial at relatively low doses.

It appears that many of these hormetic phytochemicals are typically consumed by us humans in the low-dose range, but some of these substances can be toxic in low doses, such as some of the chemicals in certain types of fungi.

There is almost an endless list of phytochemicals in plants, certainly far too many to discuss here, so let's get straight to the most researched phytochemicals that have been shown to have a hormetic benefit (see table 4.1; there are lots of others, but these are some of the better studied that we should all include in our diet).

Table 4.1: The most researched phytochemicals and their benefits

Phytochemical	*Where it's found*	*Established benefits*
Sulforaphane	Broccoli, kale, cabbage, brussel sprouts and other cruciferous vegetables	Anti-inflammatory, anti-oxidant and anti-tumour effects; neuroprotective effects; activates detoxification enzymes
Resveratrol	Grapes (and red wine!)	Anti-inflammatory, anti-oxidant and anti-tumour effects; neuroprotective effects; activates heat shock proteins
Curcumin	Turmeric (and, therefore, many curries)	Anti-inflammatory and anti-oxidant effects; neuroprotective effects; activates heat shock proteins and detoxification enzymes
Epigallocatechin gallate (EGCG), epicatechin gallate (ECG) and epigallocatechin (EGC)	Green tea (and some other types of tea)	Anti-inflammatory and anti-oxidant effects; neuroprotective effects

Phytochemical	*Where it's found*	*Established benefits*
Hydroxytyrosol	Olives, olive leaves and olive oil	Anti-inflammatory and anti-oxidant effects
Oleuropein aglycone	Olives, olive leaves and olive oil	Anti-inflammatory and anti-oxidant effects
Ferulic acid	Tomatoes, sweetcorn and rice	Anti-inflammatory and anti-oxidant effects; neuroprotective effects
Spermidine	Soybeans, natto, mushrooms, aged cheese	Anti-inflammatory and anti-oxidant effects; neuroprotective effects

Conclusion

For the vast majority of human history, we have eaten fresh, natural foods, and our biochemistry is dependent upon a steady supply of nutrients and phytochemicals from natural foods in order to function well. Our modern diets have become full of food-like substances that hijack our brains' reward systems to create the urge to overconsume them, and doing so directly wreaks havoc on our ecosystem of cells. In addition, these foods 'crowd out' a range of beneficial hormetic phytochemicals that help protect us from a wide range of diseases – a negative double whammy for our health.

The abundance of food and the ease with which to get it also keeps us in a constantly fed state. This robs us of metabolic flexibility and a number of biologically conserved mechanisms seen in many species that prevent disease and increase both healthspan and lifespan.

Implementing a low HI diet with the 80/20 rule, along with some intermittent fasting, will take you a long way towards better physical and mental health.

Visit content.mindbodybrain.com.au/document/document/40_foods.pptx to download a 40-foods per week challenge worksheet.

Chapter 5

Sculpt your brain

'Between stimulus and response there is a space.
In that space is our power to choose our response.
In our response lies our growth and our freedom.'
– Unattributed quote used by Stephen R. Covey to
summarise Viktor Frankl's essential teachings

Think of a bonsai – those miniature trees that are shaped by their pot and the pruning from the owner. In a way, our minds are like bonsai, in that they are shaped by our environment and our experiences.

Amit Goswami is a retired professor of physics from the University of Oregon and was a theoretical quantum physicist for decades. He has also written several books and is now a philosopher who started Quantum Activism Vishwalayam, an institution that runs Masters and PhD programs in the quantum science of health, prosperity and happiness in conjunction with the University of Technology, Jaipur. He said something years ago that has always stuck with me: 'We always perceive something after reflection in the mirror of memory'.

Think about that for a moment in this context: you are born with around 200 billion neurons (or nerve cells) in your brain. By the time you are two years old, you've lost around 100 billion of them through a process of 'synaptic pruning'. Just like the bonsai is shaped by its pot environment and pruning from its owner, your brain is completely shaped by your experiences. This means that your brain is a unique filter through which you view the world. And because 'We always perceive something after reflection in the mirror of memory', your past experience significantly affects how you perceive reality.

However, neuroscience has established that your brain has an enormous potential for neuroplasticity, which is its ability to change and adapt – or be sculpted. This chapter is all about sculpting your brain; it's about reshaping your brain, particularly around how you process thoughts, choose how you react to your circumstances and actually interact with the world on a daily basis.

Are you ready to sculpt your brain?

The power of self-talk

First, let's discuss the work of psychiatrist Daniel Goleman. He presents a self-talk loop that I think we can all relate to (see figure 5.1).

Figure 5.1: The self-talk loop

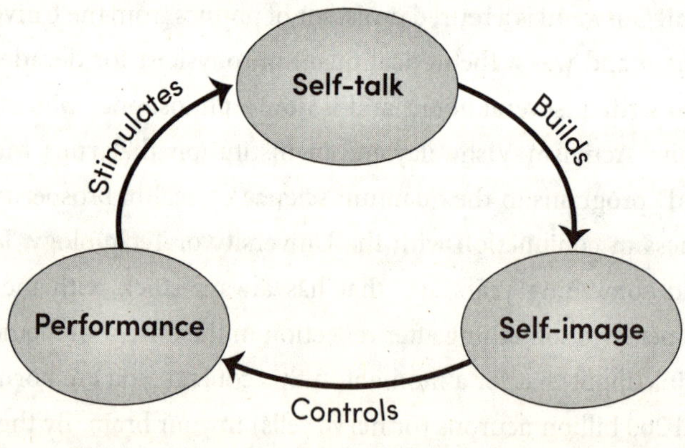

According to Goleman, this can either be a negative loop or a positive loop and, in both cases, they often become self-fulfilling prophecies. To explain this, let's take a look at the loop.

Let's imagine that you're given a challenging task to do at work. You may be familiar with the little negative voice that pops up and tells you you're not good enough – let's call this your 'Inner Gremlin'. If you pay attention to this voice, it will negatively affect how you perform at the task. Then, when you bomb out, your Inner Gremlin says to you, 'See? I told you you're shit'. In this way, the negative self-talk becomes a self-fulfilling prophecy.

Conversely, there are times when, for one reason or another, our self-talk is positive, even when we are faced with challenges. This positive voice we'll refer to as your 'Inner Sage'. Your Inner Sage might say to you, 'This is a big challenge, but you got this'. Being in this positive frame of mind, as any athletes will tell you (and research backs this up), has a significant positive effect on your performance. Then, when you nail it, your Inner Sage says, 'See? I told you that you could do it. Nice job!' (See figure 5.2.)

Figure 5.2: Your Inner Gremlin versus your Inner Sage

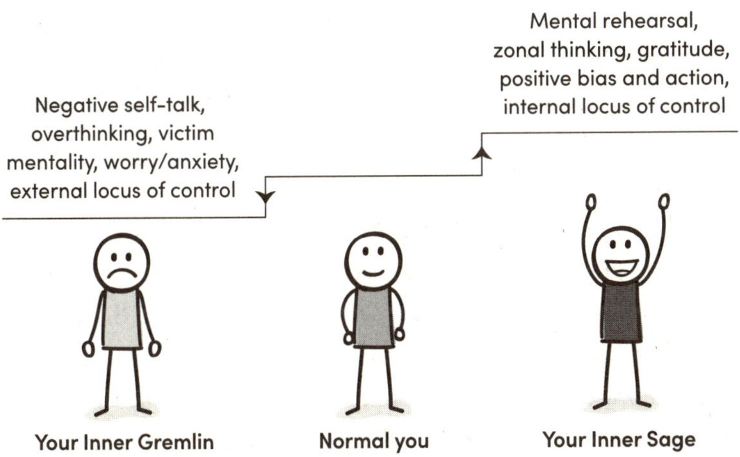

It's pretty clear from this scenario that the critical factor is the factor that we have the most influence over: our self-talk. I'm not suggesting for one minute that always having positive self-talk is easy, or that positive self-talk will solve all of your problems and turn your dreams into reality, but clearly it is influential. This is why athletes and peak performers from different domains focus so much on their self-talk, and use positive rituals and affirmations to support it, particularly in big moments.

Before we discuss what to do about this, let me tell you about a groundbreaking neuroscience experiment that has implications for us all. Back in 1995, Harvard neuroscientist Alvaro Pascual-Leone gathered a group of local volunteers who were not piano players. In the first part of the study, he taught the participants a one-handed, five-finger exercise on the piano and had them practise for two hours a day over five days. At the start of the study and at the end of each day's practice session, the participants underwent a procedure called 'transcranial magnetic stimulation' (TMS), which sends a brief magnetic pulse into the motor cortex of the brain (the part that controls bodily movement), allowing Pascual-Leone to assess the function of these neurons. The procedure mapped how much of each participant's motor cortex was dedicated to controlling the finger movements needed for the piano exercise. After a week of practice, the area of motor cortex devoted to these finger movements became bigger – basically, the brain was adapting to the stimulation of the fingers and changing accordingly.

This was a very interesting finding, but the second part of the study was pretty mind-blowing (excuse the pun). In this part, Alvaro split subjects into three groups. The first group went through the same protocol as the subjects in the first part of the study: five days of physical practice. The second group was a control group, who didn't do any practice but instead read magazines for the same amount of time that the piano players were practising. As in the first part, the physical practice group experienced changes in their motor cortex (and the control group didn't), and they performed better over the five days. But here's the kicker: there was a third group, who were shown the piece but did not physically practice. Instead, they were instructed to mentally practice the piece for the same amount of time that the first group physically practised. At the end of five days, they also developed physical changes in their brains, and their performance improved accordingly. Think about that: physical changes in the brain from mental practice!

Mental visualisation is a very powerful tool, which is why elite athletes all around the world use it to improve their performance. Let's now explore how you can use this technique in your everyday life to become a better version of yourself. This involves a 'thought experiment' where you think about those voices in your head that I mentioned earlier: your Inner Gremlin and Inner Sage.

Your Inner Gremlin and Inner Sage

Let's focus on your Inner Gremlin first. It's responsible for negative self-talk and anxious responses to situations. It tells you to press snooze when the alarm goes off, that you're the victim, that it's OK to eat crappy food or drink too much alcohol because you've had a hard day (poor you!), that you deserve better, that you're entitled to this and that, and so on. Gremlins are folkloric creatures that were said to cause aircraft malfunctions, especially during World War II. Likewise, our Inner Gremlin is responsible for cognitive malfunctions, negative self-talk, a tendency to overthink things, procrastination, a victim mentality and negative attitudes that don't serve us well. They are very emotional and hypervigilant to threats, and are supercharged by feelings of fear, shame, embarrassment and inadequacy, so they are always on the lookout for the merest hint of a situation that may trigger these emotions. So, if you've had a harsh upbringing or have faced any kind of trauma or mental illness, your Inner Gremlin can be a dominant character. While they can be useful when we're actually in danger, they're often very unhelpful in everyday life.

In the movie *Gremlins*, the small, furry creatures called 'mogwai' must never be fed after midnight, or they turn into destructive gremlins. This is a good analogy for your Inner Gremlin: you should never feed it, because then it becomes more destructive – and we feed our Inner Gremlin when we *pay attention* to it. Your attention is a very powerful thing. In Japanese psychology, it's said that your life is made up of the summation of what you pay attention to – that really deserves some serious contemplation, especially because, if you remember from earlier chapters, your brain commits cells to whatever you pay attention to.

Most people would like to get rid of their Inner Gremlin, and there are some psychotherapy approaches that try to do that, such as psychoanalytic therapy. However, there's another approach that I think of as the 'accelerator program'. This is where acceptance and commitment therapy (ACT), Morita therapy (a Japanese psychotherapy) and Stoic philosophy are all in agreement – they postulate that we are all affected by negative thoughts and attitudes as part of being human, but paying attention to these negative thoughts makes things worse. We do experience bad events, sometimes terrible events, but as Stoic philosopher Epictetus said, 'It's not what happens to you, but how you react to it that matters'. The key thing is to acknowledge that the negative or anxious thoughts are real and that they exist, but to choose to shine the light of your attention onto positive, action-oriented behaviours instead.

In the words used to summarise Viktor Frankl's teachings: 'Between stimulus and response there is a space. In that space is our power to choose our response. In our response lies our growth and our freedom'.

So, what do we do when our Inner Gremlin pops up?

First, you need to observe of your own mind and realise when you're being 'hooked' by the negative emotions or thoughts of your Inner Gremlin. Then you say to your Inner Gremlin, 'Thanks for that story you're telling me, but it's not helpful right now'. Then you take your Inner Gremlin and put it in your back pocket; it's still telling the same story, but you can't really make out what it's saying because you're no longer paying attention to it.

Instead, you consult what the Stoics referred to as your 'Sage'. The Stoics were great proponents of having a Sage – your ideal or higher self, who you could consult in challenging times or when faced with moral choices. This is what I call your 'Inner Sage'. This is the best and wisest version of you – the version that has a positive bias and takes positive action in the face of the multitude of inevitable challenges that life will throw at you. I think that every single person should have an Inner Sage.

JEV – my Inner Sage

There is an exercise for you to complete at the end of this chapter, but before you do it, let me share some stories.

My Inner Sage, who I call on when I'm challenged or faced with moral dilemmas, is called 'JEV' – his name comes from the initials of three people who I highly admire, particularly due to their courage in the face of adversity.

The 'J' in JEV stands for 'Jim Stockdale', or 'James Bond Stockdale' if you include his somewhat fitting middle name. Stockdale was a fighter pilot in the U.S. Navy and served in the Vietnam War. He was stationed on board the aircraft carrier the USS *Oriskany*. On 9 September 1965, while flying on a mission over North Vietnam, Stockdale's aircraft was struck by enemy fire, and he ejected from the aircraft and parachuted into a small village, where he was severely beaten and taken prisoner. He was held as a prisoner of war in the Hoa Lo Prison, which was dubbed the 'Hanoi Hilton' by its inmates – a sarcastic nickname given the harsh conditions of the prison camp.

Stockdale spent the next seven and a half years in that prison camp, almost four of which were spent in solitary confinement, where he was tortured routinely. As the senior naval officer in the prison, he was one of the primary organisers of prisoner resistance, and he created a shared mission and enforced a code of conduct for all prisoners, which governed their reactions to torture, their secret communications and their behaviours.

Many things have been written about the Hanoi Hilton and the importance of Jim Stockdale to the other prisoners. Former US senator John McCain, who died in 2018, was a prisoner in the Hanoi Hilton for five and a half years and went on record saying, 'Jim inspired us to do things we never believed we were capable of. Without him, I certainly wouldn't have made it out of the prison with my honor intact. We owe our lives to Jim Stockdale'. Commander Everett Alvarez Jr., the first American to be shot down and captured, said of Stockdale, 'In hindsight, it was as if he were meant to be there. It was as if God had a plan for him'.

When Stockdale was asked how he got through those seven and a half years, he was very clear. He recalled that in 1959, the U.S. Navy sent him to Stanford University to do a master's degree in international relations to prepare him for future staff jobs. Because he had some spare time on his hands, he undertook a short course in philosophy and struck up a friendship with the Dean of Humanities, Philip Rhinelander, who taught philosophy. Rhinelander thought that, being a military man, Stockdale would enjoy the teachings of the Stoic philosophers. Every week they had a meeting where they would discuss philosophy, and when Stockdale left the university,

Rhinelander gave him a copy of *The Enchiridion* by Epictetus and said, 'I think you'll be interested in this'. 'Enchiridion' means 'ready at hand' (in other words, a handbook). Epictetus is the 'E' in my JEV.

Epictetus was born a slave around the year 50 AD. It's reported that at the age of 15 he was sold at a slave auction in Rome to Epaphroditus, a secretary to Emperor Nero. Later, when Epaphroditus helped Nero complete his suicide attempt, Epictetus was freed from slavery and became a philosopher. He talked about many things, but the most important thing that Stockdale learnt from Epictetus was how to handle adversity. Stockdale recounts that when he was shot down and was parachuting into the village, he could see soldiers coming to capture him and said to himself, 'I'm leaving the world of technology and entering the world of Epictetus'.

Stockdale credits the teachings of Epictetus with helping him and his fellow prisoners survive the Hanoi Hilton, and upon his release wrote a book called *Courage Under Fire: Testing Epictetus' Doctrines in a Laboratory of Human Behaviour*.

One teaching that was particularly useful to the POWs was the idea of 'zones' in your life. Epictetus said that everything in your life sits in one of two zones: zone one contains the stuff that is within your will or your power, and zone two contains everything else. He said that we should make the best use of what is within our power, and take the rest as it happens.

Zone one contains such things as your belief systems, what you choose to be afraid of, what you choose to desire, your attitudes, your behaviours and, especially, how you choose to react to things. Zone two contains such things as your external environment, things that other people do or say, what other people think of you, workplace stress, COVID-19, the past and the future. When you are faced with challenges, Epictetus says you should 'focus on what you can control, and refuse to invest your energy in that which you can't control'.

This mindset helped the POWs deal with incredibly tough situations, and it can help us in many aspects of life. Think about the practical application of these zones: they provide a great filter for our thoughts, our focus and our energy. Think of a time when you invested your energy in some absolute dickhead, or found yourself in an overthinking vortex. How did focusing your energy on those things work out for you? Was that an awesome investment of your energy and focus, or not so good?

Ultimately, we choose where to invest our energy. Often, we invest our energy in negative things, such as worrying that someone else might be thinking ill of us, ruminating on bad stuff that happened in our past, or having anxious thoughts about situations that may never occur. Consciously choosing where to focus your energy is really important.

The 'V' in my JEV character is Viktor Frankl, whose book *Man's Search for Meaning* had a profound impact on me when I read it as a 17 year old. He was a Jewish psychiatrist who was imprisoned in Auschwitz during the Holocaust, and he obviously suffered through horrible experiences while there. In his memoirs, Frankl recounts remembering the words of Friedrich Nietzsche, 'He who has a why to live for can bear almost any how,' and how those words were so evident in Auschwitz.

Frankl noticed that the few people who survived had a very strong sense of meaning and purpose in their lives – a 'why'. What really helped Frankl endure all of the suffering was finding purpose and meaning in trying to create some good out of the horrors of what had happened. He decided to use the negative experience to help shape a new type of psychotherapy that he had been working on, expanding and refining in his head every day. He reasoned with himself that, if he didn't survive, no good would come of the whole situation and all of his friends would have died for nothing; but if he survived, he could create some good out of the terrible situation that was Auschwitz. That gave him the strength to survive.

When Frankl was released from Auschwitz, he published his manuscript on logotherapy, which has since become a very successful treatment for anxiety and depression. During his time in Auschwitz, Frankl realised that people are capable of terrible things: they can take away all of your belongings, all of your dignity, all of your pride, even all of your loved ones. They can take from you everything but one thing, which he called 'the last of human freedoms' and which is one of the key tenets of logotherapy: your ability to choose how you react to your circumstances, to choose your own attitude, to choose your own way.

Think about those words, along with the words of Epictetus and the thinking of Jim Stockdale. Those guys would have been very supportive of the notion that every day you get to choose who's in control, and what version of you you're going to bring – whether you're going to bring your Inner Gremlin or your Inner Sage into a meeting, or into your interactions with people. When you're faced with a challenge, you get to choose whether your Inner Gremlin fronts up and plays the victim, gets angry or looks for someone else to blame; or whether your Inner Sage fronts up and looks for the solution, or uses difficult situations to practise a virtue or sharpen your character, as the Stoics advised us to. And particularly when you get home from work, if you've had a stressful day, you still get to choose what version of you goes into the house to interact with your partner, with your kids.

Frankl said most of our responses are default responses to certain events or stimuli – they just kind of happen automatically. However, if you remember the quote from earlier in the chapter, his teachings can also be summarised with the words, 'Between stimulus and response there is a space. In that space is our power to choose our response'. Every day, you get to choose.

Bringing your Inner Gremlin and Inner Sage to life

In a moment, I'm going to introduce you to an exercise designed to help you bring your Inner Gremlin and your Inner Sage to life. It involves writing down their respective character strengths, and it's a great idea to draw the characters. If you have kids, this is one of the coolest things you'll ever do with them. When I did this with my kids, my little guy Oscar was only five at the time. We had just watched the movie *Inside Out* and talked about the little voices or characters inside our heads, which was a great segue to the exercise. So, if you've got kids, get them to watch that movie and then ask them to name the negative character. I asked Oscar, 'Who's the negative character, mate, who whines at his sister, who's grumpy, who doesn't want to do stuff, who stomps around?' And he looked at me and said, 'Oh yeah, that's Derek'. I asked him to go and draw Derek, as well as his Inner Sage, who he called 'Flash'. He drew them, and his sister Ceara did the same thing – but as well as drawing the characters, they also decided to do little speech bubbles. Oscar did Derek's speech bubble, and in it he wrote, 'I will crush the good ones, and I will be the king of Oscar's head.' Wow – how cool is that from a five-year-old? He's right: the negative self-talk, that Inner Gremlin, crushes the positive self-talk and becomes the king of your head, if you *choose* to pay attention to it!

Ceara's Gremlin was called 'Millie', and she drew Millie with really negative body language. The name she chose for her Inner Sage was 'Shaka', after a famous Zulu warrior, and she was very proud of Shaka. My kids use these characters a lot. They both participate in karate and compete in kumite, which is the combat form of competition. As you can imagine, even though it's a controlled sport, combat for kids is pretty stressful, particularly when they're in a competition. It was my little girl Ceara who came up with the idea that every time she stepped onto the tatami to compete, when her foot came in contact with the mat all the energy (or stress) in her body turned her into Shaka. This is similar to what many elite athletes call 'getting their game face on'. They talk about having a trigger – whether it's when they lace up their boots, put on their boxing gloves, cross the white line or get into the swimming pool – where they switch characters.

So, what will your trigger be when you go to work every day? Is it when you walk into your office? Is it just before you go to a meeting? You could mark it with a physical trigger, such as squeezing your thumb and forefinger together, which you use to remind you to connect to your Inner Sage.

When you complete the exercise, writing down your Inner Sage's character strengths and drawing the character will create a network of cells in your brain associated with this character, and every time you spend a quick ten seconds visualising your Inner Sage, it will strengthen that neural network. Remember Pascual-Leone's research: the more often you think about your Inner Sage, the stronger the network becomes entrenched in your brain, and the easier it therefore becomes to channel your Inner Sage when needed. The most important time of day to do this is when you come home, just before you go in to see your family – you need to choose what version of you will walk through that door.

OK, here's the exercise: Write down a name for your Inner Gremlin and your Inner Sage, and under each write:

- what they say first thing in the morning
- what they say when faced with a challenge
- their character traits.

When faced with a challenge, your Inner Gremlin may say things like 'I'm not good enough', 'Why me?' or 'Why do I have to do this?', and your Inner Sage responds with things like 'Bring it on' or 'I've got this'.

The really important part is the character traits. Your Inner Gremlin tends to be strong in the areas of avoidance, procrastination, pessimism, hypervigilance and self-pity, but it's really important to focus on the traits of your Inner Sage. Your Inner Sage has the character traits that you have when you're at your best, as well as some character traits that you admire in others and wish you had more of. It helps to use external role models as inspiration to create this internal role model for yourself. It's about creating 'awesome you'. Your Inner Sage is the version of you that you're going to visualise when you put Pascual-Leone's research on mental rehearsal into practice.

As you do this exercise, feel free to elaborate on your characters further to really bring them to life. What are their favourite sports teams? Favourite drinks? Favourite clothes?

Conclusion

A few years ago, I did this exercise at a workshop in Australia for one of the big banks, and a guy came up to me afterwards and said that he enjoyed it and would like to do a similar workshop for his team, who'd been under a lot of pressure. We arranged to meet and discuss it, and when we got together, he said, 'I've become a cynical bugger. I've seen a lot of speakers in my time. But you talked about two things so compellingly I started to do them. I thought I'd run an experiment'. He said the first one was the cold showers: 'That just completely transformed my morning. I used to really not be a morning person, and that has set me up for the day.' He also said, 'I used to do that game-face stuff and that mental rehearsal, the mental sculpting, when I was an athlete. I never ever thought of doing it in the workplace. I've started to do it, and it's had a massive positive impact on the workplace.'

His name is Kieren Perkins, and he's one of Australia's greatest ever swimmers. So, if this is good enough for Kieren Perkins, it's good enough for you! So, do your Inner Gremlin and Inner Sage character exercise, and choose to get your game face on – I believe it's one of the most effective ways to sculpt your brain.

Chapter 6

Recover and regenerate

'It's very important that we re-learn the art of resting and relaxing. Not only does it help prevent the onset of many illnesses that develop through chronic tension and worrying; it allows us to clear our minds, focus, and find creative solutions to problems.'
– Thich Nhat Hanh

By now you're aware that hormesis is about intermittent exposure to low-to-moderate doses of stressors, which can be toxic or lethal at high doses, in order to develop stress resistance and improvements in metabolic functioning.

One key aspect that also determines whether or not stress is good for us is the quality of our recovery, and a lot of really good research in this area comes from the world of sport and athlete performance. A number of excellent research papers have highlighted the strong similarities between workplace burnout and overtraining syndrome in athletes, with a number of common symptoms shown in table 6.1 (overleaf).

Table 6.1: Common symptoms of overtraining and burnout

Overtraining	*Burnout*
Physical performance impairment	Working capacity impairment
Tiredness	Tiredness
Irritability	Irritability
Sleep disturbance	Sleep disturbance
Sensitivity to infections	Sick absences
Cardiovascular changes	Cardiovascular changes
Hormonal changes	(Inconclusive)
Activation of inflammations	(Inconclusive)

The world of sports science is light-years ahead of workplace wellness research when it comes to managing workload or stress, and I think that we can all learn valuable lessons from this field to stay on the peak-performance side of what I call the 'performance–burnout tightrope' that many of us are walking.

In order to do that and optimise our physical and mental health, we need to get serious about two types of recovery: micro-recovery and macro-recovery.

Micro-recovery

This is all about working smarter and not harder, and making sure that we have mini-breaks throughout the day to regenerate our bodies and especially our brains. When we work constantly throughout the day, levels of the stress hormone cortisol tend to rise, and that can make us feel tired and irritable and have a negative impact on our cognitive function.

The clever way to work is in short bouts of focused work interspersed with short, high-quality breaks. Professor Cal Newport has written a lot in this area, including a great book called *Deep Work*. He suggests a number of different strategies, and my favourite is the rhythmic approach, where you chunk your work into certain time blocks and get rid of distractions, such as phone and email, to do short periods of deep work. I'm a particular fan of the pomodoro technique, where you do 25 minutes of focused work and then take a five-minute break. (I realise this isn't always possible – you may have hour-long meetings, for example – but you can use this when you have control over your work schedule.) I like this timescale because we know that there are significant changes in gene expression that occur when you sit for longer than 20 to 30 minutes at a time, and these changes affect your blood pressure and cognitive function.

The five-minute recovery periods are critical for renewing your energy and focus, and there are a few key things to do to maximise the effectiveness of this recovery period.

First, perform a 30- to 60-second movement snack. My personal favourite is a kettlebell swing, which is an exercise that engages almost every muscle in your body and fires up your metabolism. If you don't have a kettlebell, you can just sprint on the spot for 30 seconds! Why not put down this book right now and sprint on the spot as fast as you possibly can for 30 seconds – I guarantee that you will be blowing out your arse, as we Irish like to say (which means breathing very heavily). This burst of high-intensity exercise does two great things:

1. It massively increases blood flow and oxygen to the brain, which boosts your cognitive function for your next phase of work.

2. If you are stressed, it burns up stress hormones and allows your body to come back to homeostasis (biological balance). Think about it – stress hormones come from activation of our nervous system's fight-or-flight response. This prepares our bodies to fight or run away, but when we don't move, these stress hormones stay high, and we don't come back to homeostasis.

For me, this is one of the great gifts of the COVID-19 pandemic – many people report to me that the biggest barrier to doing these movement snacks during work hours is being in the office and feeling self-conscious. Because many of us now spend at least part of our time working from home, this barrier can disappear. If you are in the office and feel self-conscious, just run up a few flights of stairs, or go into the toilet cubicle and bang out 50 squats!

Once you have done your movement snack, the next part of your micro-recovery is to open up your field of vision. This is important because neuroscientist Andrew Huberman's lab showed that focusing for prolonged periods of time at a short distance (such as at a computer screen) activates the threat response in the brain. He suggests that we can offset this by widening our field of vision – be that by getting outside, looking out of a window, or just letting your field of vision expand to take in the whole office scene rather than just your computer.

The next part of your micro-recovery process is to drink a glass of water. Dehydration has a very negative effect on brain function and decision-making, and being well hydrated is important for overall metabolic health.

Lastly, I encourage you to spend one or two minutes doing some mindful breathing. There are a couple of techniques that I'm a big fan of. One is called 'box breathing': the idea is that you close your eyes and breathe into your diaphragm (into your stomach and not your chest) for a count of four (or three, or five, or whatever suits you), hold for a count of four, breathe out for four and hold for four. Repeat for four to eight cycles. U.S. Navy SEALs use this technique to control their arousal (stress) and put their brains into an optimal performance state. If you know anything about special forces soldiers, you'll know that they don't do 'fluffy bullshit', but they're very keen to do things that give them a performance edge.

An alternative to box breathing is to do a 10-second breath cycle where you breathe in for four seconds and out for six seconds (or in for three, out for seven). The longer breath out is key because it switches on your parasympathetic nervous system (the rest and digest system, the opposite to the fight-or-flight response), which calms your brain down. It's only taken us scientists 3000 years to catch up with the knowledge of yogis, who have long said that certain breathing patterns can positively influence your heart and your brain.

The idea is to do these brain-booster breaks regularly – ideally every 30 minutes, but if that's not practical, at least every hour. The corporate clients I have worked with who have implemented this strategy have reported back to me that they are more productive and have more energy, particularly in the afternoon and when they get home from work. They are then able to spend more quality time with loved ones, which is a great side effect.

Macro-recovery

Macro-recovery is all about sleep.

Most of us are big fans of sleep, and we all realise how it can make or break our day, but there is now some pretty cool sleep science to explain why it's so important for both short-term performance and mood, and long-term physical and mental health.

When you sleep, numerous restorative biological processes are activated: growth hormone is released to repair our bodies, memory is consolidated, and our brain gets rid of toxins.

Sleep can be broadly divided into rapid eye movement (REM) sleep and non-REM sleep. Most adults will enter sleep from the drowsy state into non-REM sleep and typically transition through the following stages in cycles of between 90 and 120 minutes (with four or five cycles a night):

- *Stage N1:* Your heartbeat and breathing slow, your muscles begin to relax, and there's an increase in brain waves called 'theta waves'.
- *Stage N2:* This is the biggest percentage of overall sleep, characterised by light sleep from which you can wake easily.
- *Stage N3:* This is known as deep sleep, where your heart and breathing rates drop further, growth hormone release peaks, you undergo cellular repair and your immune system strengthens.
- *REM sleep:* Your muscles become paralysed and you enter into dream state, and brain activity is markedly increased.

Something very cool also happens in REM sleep: in 2019, Dutch researchers showed that REM sleep is critical for emotional processing. During sleep, 'memory traces' of experiences from the past day are spontaneously played back, like a movie – but the brain blocks the release of the stress hormone noradrenaline (norepinephrine) during REM sleep, and so REM sleep appears to act as a kind of nightly therapy for the brain, helping to process and reduce the intensity of stressful events and negative emotions.

The Dutch researchers were able to impair this REM sleep in some subjects and showed that there was greater activation of the amygdala, the part of the brain that processes negative emotions, the next day. Because of this research and that of others, we now know that disrupting REM sleep interferes with this nightly therapy and can increase the risk of anxiety and depression.

When we sleep, all throughout the body and the brain there are processes happening to drive repair at a cellular level. For instance, we know that our cardiovascular system will attempt to repair any damage that has occurred during the day while we are asleep, and the same is true for our immune system. Our muscular system is at rest, and the endocrine (or hormone) system initiates the release of growth hormones in order to repair muscles and make them stronger. Our endocrine system also undergoes widespread repair when we are asleep, and the brain consolidates its learning habits and memories. Obviously, sleep is very important for our mood, and I think most people get that.

Most of us have heard of the body's lymphatic system, which gets rid of waste products from cellular metabolism on a daily basis. Just through the process of staying alive, cells produce a lot of waste, which can be toxic. However, we don't have a lymphatic system in the brain, so it has puzzled scientists for decades how the brain gets rid of its waste products. Then, a few years ago, some scientists discovered what has been named the 'glymphatic system', which is a system for transporting cellular waste products that is built around our cardiovascular system.

It turns out that when we are asleep, the spaces around our nerve cells in the brain actually become bigger, and the nerve cells then dump their waste products into this space, which then connects to our glymphatic system. This then transports this waste out through the blood–brain barrier and into the lymphatic system, which disposes these waste products along with the rest of our cellular waste through the liver and kidneys. Pretty cool, huh?

Our brain health is heavily dependent upon this glymphatic system – and this system is very dependent upon us getting sufficient sleep. The glymphatic system is used to distribute important molecules such as glucose, amino acids, lipids (or fats) and growth factors, all of which contribute to a healthy brain.

When you don't sleep well, your brain doesn't get these critical molecules in sufficient amounts, and there is also a build-up of metabolic waste products. Together, these factors predispose you to a whole host of neurological disorders, including Alzheimer's disease and mental health issues.

A systematic review published in 2013 looked at the relationship between sleep disturbances, anxiety and depression and found that the relationship was bidirectional – poor sleep can cause anxiety and depression, and anxiety or depression can cause poor sleep... and the downward spiral continues.

Chronic poor sleep can also dramatically increase your risk of obesity, type 2 diabetes, cardiovascular disease and a host of cancers.

In addition to these long-term impacts, even one or two nights of poor sleep can have numerous short-term consequences:

- *Cognitive performance:* We know that even moderate sleep restriction of up to two hours less than you would normally have has a very detrimental impact on performance. Studies have shown that people who are moderately deprived of sleep perform worse in driving tests and cognition tests than people who are over the legal drinking limit.
- *Stress responsivity:* A bad night's sleep affects your stress response systems, which release higher levels of cortisol into your bloodstream. You start the next day more susceptible to stress, which subsequently interferes with your sleep that night, and this then turns into an awful cycle of increased stress that lots of us will recognise.

- *Hunger:* When we have poor sleep, levels of ghrelin (our major hunger hormone) are increased the following day, which drives us to eat more food – and, because cortisol is higher, we tend to go for sugary, salty and fatty foods.
- *Physical activity:* Poor sleep reduces the amount of leptin that is released in our brains. This hormone exerts a powerful effect on voluntary physical activity, so lower leptin levels mean that we're more likely to sit more and less likely to exercise. This means that we're less able to handle the stresses of the day (because exercise is a great stress-buster) and more likely to reach for alcohol or comfort food in the evening to take the edge off, which both negatively impact our sleep that night – and it's groundhog day!
- *Small testes:* Yes, gentlemen – smaller nuts! A group of researchers from the University of Southern Denmark has found that sleep-deprived men actually have lower testosterone levels and reduced sperm counts. To add insult to injury, they also experience observable testicular shrinkage!

Now that we know how important sleep is, let's talk about sleep hygiene, because there are a lot of things we can do that will significantly improve our sleep. Following are the key sleep hygiene habits.

Caffeine

Many people love a good cup of coffee or tea, but it's important to remember that caffeine is a stimulant. It's a well-known enhancer of cognitive performance, and they give it to fighter pilots in times of war to keep them awake. But how quickly does it wear off? For the average person, the half-life of caffeine is about six hours, which means that six hours after a cup of coffee or tea, half of it – around 40 milligrams for a cup of coffee – is still in your system. This can vary greatly, though – from two to twelve hours – because some people are fast metabolisers and some are slow metabolisers.

So, when it comes to how much you can drink without it affecting your sleep, the answer is a product of how much you drink and how fast you metabolise it. Your body weight and which variant of the gene CYP1A2 you possess are the main factors affecting processing speed. However, if you have poor sleep, a pretty good general rule is to try to have your last caffeine exposure eight to ten hours before bed, and aim for no more than 250 milligrams of caffeine daily. There are many websites where you can check the caffeine content of various drinks.

Remember that, as well as being present in coffee, tea and energy drinks, caffeine is also found in most diet sodas and, to a lesser extent, chocolate as well. If you're having multiple exposures of caffeine through the day, it's building up in your system – and if you're a standard metaboliser and have more than four exposures spread across the day on a daily basis, you will have caffeine in your brain at stimulant levels 24/7, 365 days a year!

Alcohol

I'm Irish and ex-military, and I like a tipple – and we all know that alcohol can help you unwind before sleep. However, more than two standard alcoholic drinks (or even less for smaller people) interferes with the quality of your sleep by reducing the amount of time you spend in restorative REM sleep. Remember research has shown that disturbed REM sleep interferes with proper emotional processing and heightens amygdala activity the next day. Consuming no alcohol is best for sleep, but if you do like a tipple, try to limit it to one or two standard drinks.

Marijuana also interferes with REM sleep, which is why excessive use of it can make some people susceptible to mood issues.

Exercise

Earlier I covered all of the awesome positive effects of exercise. Another positive effect is that it induces slow-wave sleep patterns later in the day. This means that when you exercise regularly, you're more likely to get to sleep in the evening. Recent studies suggest that morning exercise may have a more beneficial effect on sleep at night than afternoon exercise – and if you do it in the morning, that shit gets done! Let's face it – we've all had days when we have the best intentions of going to the gym or doing some other form of exercise later in the day, and then life gets in the way. Morning exercise is the way to go.

Routine

According to sleep psychologists, routine is probably the most important factor for sleep quality. One of the most effective ways to sabotage your sleep is to mess with your circadian rhythm by changing the times when you go to bed and wake up. A plethora of research papers have been published showing that when you disrupt your circadian rhythm, you mess with a host of bodily functions, which impacts negatively on both your sleep and your cellular health. The strong recommendation from sleep scientists is to try to go to bed at the same time every night (or very close to it) and, even more importantly it seems, get up at the same time. I know this is not good news for most people, but try to avoid those late nights and long lie-ins on the weekend. Going to bed at roughly the same time and getting up at the same time will ensure that your circadian cycle is regular, and that will dramatically improve your sleep.

Digital sunset

One of the biggest scourges of modern living when it comes to sleep is screen time. It's been well established that if you interact with a device that emits blue light within an hour of going to bed, your level of melatonin (your sleep hormone) drops by around 30 per cent. This means you're less likely to get to sleep straight away, you're more likely to have disturbed sleep, and the sleep you do get is not going to be as restorative.

The key action you can take here is that, half an hour before you go to bed, you make sure to turn off all screens. Ideally, you would have your mobile phone out of your bedroom. If your response to this is, 'But it's my alarm clock', buy a $10 alarm clock, you tight-arse! If your mobile phone is beside your bed, your brain remains hypervigilant, saying to you, 'Someone could be texting, or liking that Instagram post – we should check!' The best solution is to ban all screens from the bedroom.

Try to avoid watching television or doing work in bed. Give yourself 30 minutes minimum for the brain to perform an essential wind-down without exposure to blue light. This is an ideal time to do meditation or box breathing, yoga or stretching, or just read a novel. Think about it – when you read a novel, you've got to create all these characters in your head, and your brain needs to go on this narrative journey. It's actually a really useful mindfulness activity. A number of executives I work with have told me that when they started reading novels at night, their sleep improved significantly; this makes perfect sense because you're giving the brain the ability to decompress before you go to sleep. The brain needs mental stillness before sleep.

If you do need to work late at night, there are some devices in the technology world that can help you with sleep. The program f.lux will change a lot of the light from your device from blue to orange, which will look at bit strange at first, but the orange light will not have that negative impact on melatonin in the brain that blue light has. Another option to combat the blue screen is to use orange-filter sunglasses, which filter out the blue light.

Sleep environment

Another factor is the levels of light noise and temperature in your bedroom. First, try to make the room as dark as possible. A recent British study showed that the best sleep occurs when you can't even see the wall opposite to you in your room. Also, try to make the environment quiet; if you live in a noisy neighbourhood, perhaps use earplugs.

Most people are surprised to hear that the ideal temperature for sleeping is 16°C to 19°C (61°F to 66°F). Lots of people have their bedrooms too warm for optimal sleep. To get to sleep, your core body temperature has to drop. This is actually why having a hot bath helps with sleep – although this may seem counterintuitive, when you have a hot bath your core body temperature reduces to try to even out your body temperature, and that helps you to go to sleep.

The final sleep hygiene factor is that your brain needs to know your bedroom is a sleep sanctuary – it's where you go to sleep (and, if you're lucky, to get a bit of oofy-magoofty every now and then!). It's not a place for watching television, doing work, for mobile phones, or for arguments – it needs to be a sanctuary.

Conclusion

Above all, don't worry about sleep. Watching the clock never helps.

That said, if you can't get to sleep after about 20 minutes, it's best to get out of bed and go into a different room to read a book, breathe, meditate or colour in, and then return to bed when you feel tired. Likewise, if your mind is busy with all the things you have to do, get out of bed and make a list, then return to bed and think of something relaxing and pleasant.

So, here's my challenge if you'd like to have better sleep: run a two-week experiment where you do as many of these things as possible. I pretty much guarantee that both your sleep and mental fitness will improve. If it doesn't work, troll me on social media!

Lastly, if you have serious sleep problems (such as insomnia), I highly recommend cognitive behaviour therapy for insomnia (CBT-I). There are several app- and web-based programs for this, and it has been shown to be more effective than sleeping tablets for those with serious sleep problems; so, if that's you, give it a try.

The big takeaway is that we need to think of ourselves the way that athletes do and get serious about recovery, because it can be the make-or-break factor in the fast-faced lives that we lead today. Our hunter-gatherer genome is programmed to go hard in bursts and rise to intermittent challenges, but recover effectively when it gets the chance – yin and yang, work and recover.

Chapter 7

Connect through the power of the tap code

'Everybody needs a tap code ... Everybody needs a set of individuals in their life that they can count on.'
– Dennis Charney

Our brains are fundamentally social organs, and we need to have a range of social connections in order to keep our brains healthy. You may have heard of the Blue Zones: the areas around the world that have the highest number of centenarians (people who live to 100 years old or more). It turns out that one of the things that they all have in common, besides being physically active and eating a healthy diet, is that they have very strong social networks. The opposite of this is being lonely, and it turns out that loneliness has around the same negative impact on your longevity as smoking cigarettes or not doing any exercise.

There's an old saying that 'it takes a village to raise a child', and many of us will have fond memories of growing up in streets or villages where people would drop into your home randomly, and everyone was there to support and look out for each other. In modern societies, a lot of this 'community spirit' is being eroded. Many people now don't know their neighbours, let alone the people down the street, yet we have a multitude of connections on Facebook and Instagram. I often go out for dinner with my family and see tables of people who are on their phones but hardly engaging with each other. It turns out that the pervasive use of mobile phones and social media has made us more digitally connected but less physically connected.

Research from 2016 revealed that smartphone users check their phone an average of 85 times a day. Other research showed that 91 per cent of smartphone users report never leaving home without their phone, and a ludicrous 46 per cent said they couldn't live without their phone. This is particularly concerning when you consider the emerging data around smartphone use and our social interactions and mental health. A 2014 study showed that when a smartphone was visibly present on a table, conversations between people were much more superficial, with lower levels of empathy and feelings of interpersonal connectedness. The researchers suggested that this was due to the smartphone distracting the attention of the people at the table and thereby undermining the character and depth of conversations. Other studies have highlighted the association between increased smartphone use and poor mental health, with increasing phone use being strongly associated with declining mental health, especially in teenage girls. US data shows a shocking rise in both suicide rates and hospital admissions for self-harm in teenage girls since the advent of social media, and 2017 data from the Royal Society for Public Health showed that Instagram, Facebook, Snapchat and Twitter use has negative impacts around sleep, bullying, anxiety, depression, loneliness, body image and fear of missing out (FOMO) in British 14- to 24-year-olds.

The importance of real social connections was made really obvious by a famous study of data collected over the last few decades in the US town of Framingham. This is one of the most studied towns on earth, with a number of studies following tens of thousands of people over decades. These people have regular visits to their GP to get poked and prodded, they answer regular questions about their health and wellbeing, and are followed up over decades to see what impacts their lifestyles have on measures such as chronic disease. One of the studies from this cohort found that blood pressure has a significant impact on your risk of developing heart disease. Another study from Framingham showed that obesity 'spreads' in a social network – if one of more of your friends becomes obese, it significantly increases your risk of becoming obese yourself in the next six months. Interestingly, this study did not find the same effect within families, showing that your friendship groups affect you the most.

The same researchers of the obesity study realised that they had a whole heap of data on not just health measures but also levels of happiness. So, they analysed happiness through the lens of social networks, because they had all of that data on how people were connected socially. What they found was staggering: if you have a happy friend who you catch up with in person at least once a month, they increase your chances of being happy by around 15 per cent. The researchers even found that your happiness can be affected by the happiness of people who are three degrees removed form you in that social network – if your friend's friend's friend is happy, it will have a positive knock-on effect on your happiness. The catch is that they have to be real social connections that meet face to face at least once a month, not digital 'friends'.

The Hanoi Hilton and the tap code

I now want to tell a story that I think brings this home really, really strongly. In chapter 5, I told a story about the Vietnam War and the brutal prisoner of war camp that the inmates ironically nicknamed the 'Hanoi Hilton'. I talked about Jim Stockdale, one of the most senior officers in the Hanoi Hilton and a personal hero of mine, who used the teachings of Epictetus – specifically, that we should focus on that which we can control and refuse to invest energy in that which we cannot control – to help himself and his fellow inmates endure years of imprisonment.

Many of the inmates in the Hanoi Hilton were tortured, especially Stockdale and a couple of other senior officers, and the edict given to the American Forces at the time was 'death before dishonor' – meaning if you are interrogated, it is better to die than dishonour your country by telling the enemy what they want to know. Stockdale was one of the first to get tortured, and he refused to tell his captors what they wanted to know, so they broke his back through torture and threw him into a cell with the other senior officers.

As Stockdale was lying there convalescing, he suggested to the other officers that they needed to change the mission, because the current mission was likely to get them all killed or severely maimed. He said that if they agreed to change the mission, he would take responsibility for it, and he would be voluntarily court-martialled if they ever got out.

They agreed on a new mission: to 'return with honor'. This meant that when you get tortured, you resist as much as you can; but when you've reached your limit, you tell the enemy what they want to know, but you also try to sprinkle in misinformation with real information to deceive the enemy.

The other officers agreed, and they spread the new mission to the other inmates along with a set of values or behaviours. One was unity, the power of 'we'. Stockdale told his fellow prisoners that no-one would get through this alone; they needed to band together to get through this, and they needed to return with their honour intact.

He also talked about having brutal honesty, first with yourself and then with everyone else. This meant that if you cracked during interrogation and gave information to the enemy, you had to be honest and tell people, because they needed to know what the enemy actually knew. Another of their values was 'second chances'. Stockdale told them that everybody in there would screw up, but everybody deserves a second chance.

A few years into their captivity, one of the guards let it slip that they were going to start putting the American POWs into solitary confinement to try to break them. The POWs quickly talked about what they could do about this new development and one of them remembered an old instructor teaching him something called the 'tap code', which they had used to communicate with each other through the walls of prison camps during World War II. It is a way of organising all the letters of the alphabet in a grid fashion (see figure 7.1). The senior officers realised that this would be very valuable to them, and they taught everybody the tap code and a shorthand to go with it.

Figure 7.1: The tap code

TAP CODE	1	2	3	4	5
1	A	B	C/K	D	E
2	F	G	H	I	J
3	L	M	N	O	P
4	Q	R	S	T	U
5	V	W	X	Y	X

Stockdale said to everybody, 'Get on the wall. Learn the tap code and share information. Help each other. Support each other. Remind each other of the mission and each POW's role in that mission.' He told them that every time someone was interrogated, when they came back into their cell, to get on the wall and tap to them – tell him that you love him and that you're here for him.

I was very fortunate to interview a Hanoi Hilton survivor called Lee Ellis on my podcast. He told me that the mission, the values and especially the tap code created a powerful culture and unshakable bond among the POWs. Many of the prisoners did extended time in solitary confinement – three and a half years in the case of Jim Stockdale – and Ellis said it was the tap code and overall culture that helped them all get through it.

Towards the end of the war, the Vietcong started trading American POWs for concessions from the Americans. They told the prisoners in the Hanoi Hilton that they were going to release them and that they could go home – but the culture was so strong that the prisoners refused to leave unless the Vietcong let them out in the order in which they came in.

Dennis Charney is a neuropsychologist and was part of a team that interviewed many of the POWs once they were released. He said that lifelong friendships were struck up in the Hanoi Hilton between guys who had never met each other face to face, because they were in the cell next to each other or the cell across the corridor and tapped to each other to help each other through their darkest times.

This is the power of social connectedness. We now know from research that one of the biggest predictors of whether a Vietnam War veteran went on to develop PTSD, anxiety or depression was whether or not they had social support networks that they used. Those soldiers who talked about their issues to supporting friends or family experienced much less PTSD and fared much better than those who bottled stuff up.

Many men around my age (50-ish) were brought up in a culture of 'big boys don't cry' – and it's utter bullshit. What we now know is that if you have a genuine 'Are you okay?' conversation with someone (which I now call a 'tap code conversation'), oxytocin and vasopressin are released in *both* people's brains. These two hormones are heavily involved in love, empathy and social bonding, but they are also both very potent anti-stress hormones.

This is what I love about Stockdale's idea of 'getting on the wall' – it takes two people, one of whom is struggling and the other who is helping – but both of their brains release these powerful anti-stress hormones because of that social connection. So, it's a beautiful symbiotic relationship. We know from other research that people who have an altruistic social interest in others improve their own mental health, and it turns out there's a whole heap of neuroscience behind altruism. We are hardwired to connect with and help others. In the words of Dennis Charney, 'Everybody needs a tap code'.

Conclusion

I'm a big fan of writing down your 'tap code gang'. This gang includes two sets of people. The first set is the people in your life, whether it's at work or at home, who you think you could reach out to if you were struggling mentally. The second set of people is equally important – they are people in your life who you think might be struggling, who could use a tap on the shoulder and an 'Are you okay?' conversation. This is about 'getting on the wall', in Stockdale's words. In one of the top five most popular TED Talks of all time, Brené Brown talks about the power of vulnerability, of opening up to others. As she points out, the word 'courage' comes from the Latin word 'cor', which means 'heart' – it takes courage to tell your story with your whole heart.

People who are struggling with mental health issues often don't reach out because they don't want to be a burden. What we now know from this research is you're not being a burden – if you find the courage to tell your story to someone, you're actually giving them an opportunity to improve their mental health.

So, if you're struggling, it's about finding the courage to reach out and tell your story. And if you've got your shit together mentally, it's about looking around to see who, in your little corner of the universe, could use a tap code conversation.

Chapter 8

Make the shift

'We are what we repeatedly do.
Excellence, then, is not an act, but a habit.'
– Will Durant

Nothing changes if nothing changes! Many of us know what we need to do but just aren't doing it, or are only partially doing it. We might do well for a while, but then we revert to type. That's why this last chapter is all about actioning your life, closing what I call the 'knowing–doing gap' and translating all of this knowledge into action.

Behaviour change is hard, or we'd all be in great shape and kicking goals. So, I want to make it EASIER for you with this mnemonic; each letter represents a key component of successful behaviour change:

- E: explore your reasons why
- A: accountability partners
- S: scaffold your goals
- I: imagery
- E: environment
- R: rituals and ritual boards.

E: explore your reasons why

Many, many philosophers throughout history have talked about the power of purpose. Ancient philosophers such as Socrates, Aristotle and Plato talked about it. Friedrich Nietzsche said, 'He who has a why to live for can bear almost any how', and that heavily influenced Viktor Frankl, who wrote amazing books on meaning and purpose. In chapters 5 and 7, I talked about and the Hanoi Hilton, Jim Stockdale and the mission to 'return with honor'. Even modern-day psychologists, psychotherapists and motivational speakers highlight purpose, such as Anthony Robbins, who says that if you find your why, you'll find your way.

Hopefully, while you've been reading this book, you've been thinking about implementing some of the tools discussed and making some changes in your life. If so, it's really useful for you to look at the research of Professors Edward Deci and Richard Ryan. They are psychologists who have studied tens of thousands of people on behaviour change journeys across 30-plus years. They've studied people who have needed to change a range of different health behaviours, including alcoholics, drug addicts and people who need huge amounts of weight loss. They have developed a continuum of human motivation under the umbrella of self-determination theory (see figure 8.1). Through numerous rigorous research studies, they have identified different phases of human motivation – from people who have a complete lack of motivation (known as 'amotivation') all the way through to people who are intrinsically motivated, where they engage in a behaviour because they enjoy it, or it's a challenge, or they want to master it.

They have found that when people begin their behaviour change journeys, they often move from the 'amotivation' phase into the 'other-determined extrinsic motivation' phase – the form of motivation that is driven by things such as rewards ('I'll buy myself something if I achieve my goal'), guilt ('I shouldn't smoke or drink so much alcohol') or coercion (someone nagging them to change). What Deci and Ryan have shown is that this phase of motivation is really good to get you started, but ultimately the vast majority of people who stay in this phase fail. These are the yo-yo dieters, the people who lose weight and then put it back on. These are the people who get fit, then get unfit; the people who stop drinking, smoking or taking drugs, then start again.

Figure 8.1: Self-determination theory

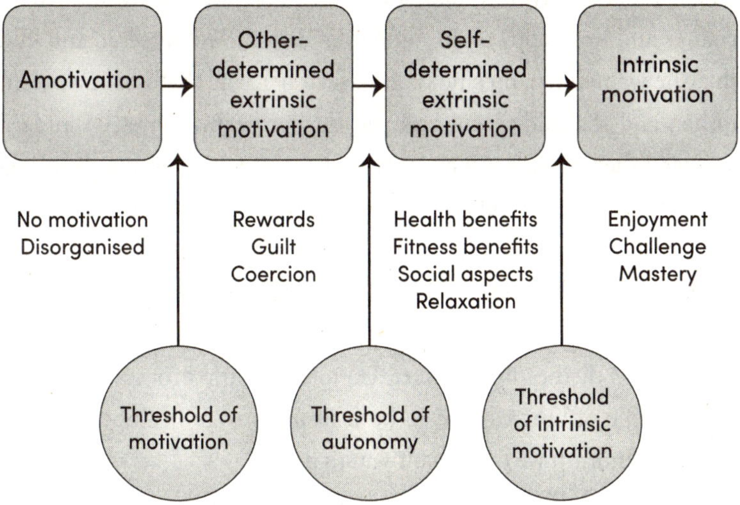

Deci and Ryan have shown that the vast majority of people who succeed cross what's called the 'threshold of autonomy' – they find their own reasons why it's important for them to change at an emotional level. Why will your life be better when you've achieved this goal – not for anybody else, but for you? What are the real emotional drivers for you to achieve this goal?

As mentioned earlier, the highest form of motivation is intrinsic motivation, where you do something for enjoyment, for the challenge or in pursuit of mastery. The great thing to know is that you don't ever need to get there (although it's a massive bonus if you do). You just need to find your why.

Here's a story that emphasises the importance of this. A year or two before writing this book, I was walking down the street in Melbourne, and this lady came out of nowhere, grabbed me and said, 'Paul Taylor, you made me cry in front of about 300 people'. I started to apologise, but she laughed and said, 'No, no, no, it's got a happy ending'. Basically, I had been talking at an event she attended about behaviour change, and I asked if anybody had something that they really wanted to change and was happy to do some role-play. She volunteered and said that she wanted to stop smoking. I asked her why that was important to her, and she said that it was bad for her health – pretty standard answer. I then asked her why it was important for her to stop smoking at a deep emotional level, and she burst into tears and said, 'The reason that I want to stop smoking is my little boys came into my room this weekend in floods of tears. The older brother, who is eight, had found from a TV ad that smoking causes lung cancer, and he knew that my mother had died of lung cancer. He told his little brother that I was going to die of lung cancer, so both of them were in floods of tears saying, "Mummy, we don't want you to die"'.

And I said, 'Bingo, there's your why. You need to find a way to remember your why, particularly when you're struggling'. I advised her to take it day by day, because smoking is very hard to give up. I advised her to look at herself in the mirror every morning and say, 'JFT (just for today), I'm not going to smoke'.

Back on the street in Melbourne, she showed me her foot – she'd had 'Remember Your Why' tattooed on her damned foot, along with 'CM' and 'LM', the initials of her two little boys. How cool is that?

She told me that every morning, she got up, stood in the shower, looked at her foot and said, 'Just for today, I'm not going to smoke – for my little boys'. She started wearing open-top shoes to work. She had a packet of cigarettes in her bag, and she made a pact with herself: If she really wanted to smoke, she could, but she had to look at her foot first and think about her little boys. She said that on numerous occasions, she went to have a smoke, and she just looked at her foot and put the cigarettes back in her bag.

That's a pretty cool story, I think you'll agree. I'm not suggesting that you go and get your foot tattooed, but I am suggesting that if you have a health goal, you really think about your why, and about why the goal is important to you on an emotional level. Then, work out how you are going to remind yourself of that on a daily basis.

To help with this process, there's a great evidence-based tool from the world of motivational interviewing (a well-established coaching process) that can help you to get clear on your reasons why it's important to change your behaviour: it's called a 'decisional balance sheet'.

You can see in table 8.1 overleaf a real-life example from an old client of mine called Richard. Richard was 55 and a successful executive, but he was overweight, unfit and starting to develop chronic disease. He wanted to get healthy again, so I asked him to fill out a decisional balance sheet. In this process, you write down the advantages and the disadvantages linked to both changing your behaviour and not changing your behaviour.

Think about your own situation as you read through Richard's example. If you look at the top right cell, this often contains what I call your 'concrete boots of habit' – the habits that are dragging you down and preventing you from taking action. In the bottom left cell, you'll often find your fears, apprehensions and automatic negative thoughts that can get in the way of change.

Once you've completed your decisional balance sheet, take some time to reflect on it. The top left and bottom right cells represent two future versions of you: top left is where you're headed if you don't sort your shit out, and the bottom right is what your life could be like. The deciding factor on where you'll end up is *you* and the accumulation of the choices that you make every single day.

Table 8.1: Richard's decisional balance sheet

	Disadvantages	*Advantages*
No change	• Health deteriorates • Economic cost of health • Can't play with kids • Burden on my family • Continue to feel isolated • Low confidence/ self-esteem	• I won't have to put in so much effort • I will have more free time • I won't be uncomfortable • I can just be me
Change	• Exercise makes me feel uncomfortable • Lots of effort is required • My genetics get in the way • Time factor • I will only fail again	• Improved self-esteem and confidence • Feel better • More energy • Enhanced mood and sex life • Easier to play with the kids • Better role model

Next, let's talk about breaking your goals up into manageable chunks.

A: accountability partners

You've probably heard the old adage, 'A problem shared is a problem halved'. This refers to the importance of social support. A multitude of research suggests that when people enlist the help of others, or go on a shared journey, they will be more successful. You've probably experienced this yourself – perhaps when getting fit with a partner or buddy, or going on some sort of health kick with someone else.

These 'accountability partners' help to keep you on track when your motivation wanes, and you step in to help them as well. That's why I'm a big fan of getting someone else to go on a shared journey with you, whether that's a partner, a friend or your kids. In the process of writing this book, my twelve year old, Oscar, was a great accountability partner for me, because he'd drag me out for a morning run when I was prioritising work – and I never regretted going for that run, because it re-energised me.

There's something else to bear in mind: if you live with a spouse or partner and you're going on a health journey that they don't want to accompany you on – whether it's stopping smoking, getting fit or losing weight – have a conversation with them at the start and ask them nicely not to be a saboteur! Often, if partners smoke, drink or don't exercise, and one of them starts to change their behaviour, it makes the other person feel guilty and probably a little bit ashamed of themselves, even if it's just on a subconscious level. The best way for them to feel better about themselves is to get you to re-engage in that old behaviour so they can justify their own behaviour.

S: scaffold your goals

If reaching your goal is more than a month away, a really useful strategy to keep you on track is to create a scaffold for your goal, like a builder does when they are building a house. Let's say that I'm working with you to help you lose 15 kilograms over the next three or four months. I'd say, 'That's great. Now, write that goal down and forget about it for now. I want you to focus on what you are going to do in the next month – what does that weight loss look like?' Then we'd take that monthly goal and break it down further into weekly mini-goals.

I call these 'weekly waypoints'. When I was a helicopter navigator in the military, if we wanted to get from point A to point B, we'd create a map for how to get there. On this route, we'd program a number of waypoints so that we could check to see if we were on track or not. If we were, great; if we had been blown off track by the wind, we'd adjust the next leg.

The reason it's great for you to have these weekly waypoints is because your brain needs feedback on whether what you're doing is or isn't working, and the timeframe of a week is a great psychological reset for humans ('I'll start next Monday!'). Your frontal lobes – the parts of your brain that drive your behaviour – aren't very good at projecting too far off into the future to modify your behaviour to achieve a goal. They're much better at focusing on shorter-term goals, which is why it helps to break the final goal into monthly goals and weekly waypoints.

The trick, then, is to review the week every Sunday and give yourself a score out of ten. Had a shit week? That's OK, but what went wrong? This is not about beating yourself up, but rather about being your own scientist so that you can tweak your experiment in an iterative way. If you have scored a three, where did the wheels start to come off, and how can you avoid that next week? Likewise, if you scored an eight, nine or ten – why was that? What things did you do early that week to start the ball rolling, and how can you replicate that result next week?

I: imagery

Let's talk about using your amazing brain to mentally rehearse your success.

If you talk to any world-class athlete, the chances are that they will do some form of mental imagery. It is also one of the 'big four' aspects of mental toughness that the United States Armed Forces are currently trained in (goal orientation, self-talk, mental rehearsal and arousal control) – and for very good reason, because it works.

Professor David Kavanagh from Queensland University of Technology has teamed up with researchers from the University of Plymouth to develop and test a process called 'functional imagery training', which involves the use of personalised, emotionally driven, goal-directed mental imagery to plan health behaviours, anticipate obstacles that may come up and mentally try out solutions based on previous successes.

I recommend that you use imagery along with your Inner Sage (discussed in chapter 5) and spend a few minutes each morning planning out your day, asking yourself the following questions and seeing yourself carry out these actions in your mind's eye:

- What healthy behaviours are you going to do today?
- Just as importantly, what are you not going to do today?
- What are some obstacles that may get in the way of your plans, and how will you avoid them?
- Visualise yourself in a challenging situation, and ask yourself 'What would my Inner Sage do right now?'

A similar process was championed by the Stoic philosophers, who said that you should imagine your day and anticipate what sort of challenges and difficult people and circumstances you might encounter, so that you will be prepared for them.

The mental imagery can also be used when you are procrastinating or are faced with temptation: 'What would my Inner Sage do right now'? In psychology, this is known as 'self-distancing', and it's been shown to improve your decision-making by creating some space between the emotional pull and the event itself, enabling you to view it more objectively. The imagery of your Inner Sage will give you some added inspiration.

E: environment

Ensure that you set up your environment to help you succeed. For example, I keep a kettlebell right beside my desk to make it easier for me to do regular movement snacks when working. There are a number of things that you can do to support your own journey, with one key rule: set up your environment to make it easier to do positive (or healthy) behaviours and harder to do negative (or unhealthy) behaviours.

Here are some examples of positive changes you can make to your environment:

- Set your exercise clothes out at the end of your bed each evening so that it's easy to put them on in the morning.
- Keep a gym bag in your car.
- Put heathy foods at the front of your fridge and pantry so you're more likely to reach for them while hungry.
- Leave a piece of exercise equipment beside your desk to trigger you to do movement snacks.
- Keep your phone out of the bedroom (buy an alarm clock!) so you can take a few minutes to mentally imagine your day before you receive any external inputs (such as news, emails or text messages).

- Only buy as much alcohol as you need, and don't keep a supply in the house, meaning you actually need to go somewhere to get it each time you want to drink.
- Don't keep shit food in the house – and don't try to get around this by making excuses that the shit food you like is actually for another family member.
- Schedule work and breaks in your calendar, rather than just on a to-do list.

Making sure that you set your environment up to help you succeed is key in helping you build healthy habits that lead to long-term behaviour change.

R: rituals and ritual boards

Rituals are the processes by which you achieve your goals, and it's much more important to focus on them than on the outcome. Darren Hardy is a prolific author who talks about bookends for your day. He notes that we have much greater control over the start and the end of our days than we do the rest of our day, so setting really good rituals for the start and the end of the day has a huge influence on the success of that day.

If you want to have an awesome tomorrow, it starts with tonight. It starts with having productive evening rituals such as 'I'm not going to drink alcohol tonight', or 'I'm going to implement good sleep hygiene practices'. Both of these ensure that you have a good sleep so you'll wake up refreshed, and then you're more likely to do your morning rituals, such as a workout and a cold shower, which are going to set you up for a productive day.

I came across the concept of rituals just over ten years before writing this book. I had entered an event called 'White Collar Boxing', which was a charity boxing event. The idea was for white-collar professionals who hadn't boxed before to undergo 12 weeks of boxing training and then put their new-found skills on the line against a fellow white-collar boxer in a big charity evening event. You had to sell two tables worth of tickets, and the money raised would go to charity. It was a black-tie event, with a three-course meal and unlimited drinks for spectators. Your friends and colleagues would come along to enjoy the evening and support you – or, if you have friends like mine, they'd cheer on your opponent!

I loved the whole journey and managed to win my fight, and sometime later they ran a 'night of champions' for people who had won before. This was a pretty clever marketing strategy, because they knew that you were able to sell tickets if you'd done it before, and if you'd won, you'd likely be up for another go.

My wife, Carly, came along to support me. I won my fight, and when she saw me afterwards she said, 'Well done, but you're not going to do this again, are you?' I quickly recognised that this was of those questions that's not actually a question, so I thought I'd be clever and answer a question with another question: 'Well, what's the problem?' I said.

'I'll tell you the problem', came the reply. 'The problem is that you're now 40. The problem is that you've got two kids. The problem is you're a neuroscientist who talks about the brain, and you're getting your head punched. It's a bit incongruent, don't you think?'

Bugger! Get out of that one!

That night, I realised that this was the end of my boxing escapades; I was really enjoying it, but I realised deep down that she was right. I was completely conflicted, though, because I enjoyed it so much. A few weeks later, I went to Carly and said, 'You know this boxing thing? I want to become a professional boxer.' She laughed, and then she said, 'Oh my God, you're serious.'

'Just hear me out', I said. 'Since you've said I can't box, I've been obsessing about boxing. I'm waking up in the middle of the night thinking about boxing. I'm walking down the street thinking about it, I'm thinking about it in meetings, and I cannot get it out of my head. I've got a massive itch, and I need to scratch it, and I think the only way I can scratch it is to take this to its logical conclusion and have a professional fight. But I just want one professional fight. I want to experience the journey, and if you let me do this, I'll hang my gloves up, and I'll never even spar again.'

Carly eventually agreed, and I started training. Being an exercise physiologist, I knew that I couldn't just start training like a professional boxer right from the get-go. I knew I had to create a graded exercise program with progressive overload. Most professional boxers have a ten-week camp. If they've kept themselves in good shape and they're coming off a recent fight, maybe they'll do an eight-week camp; if they need more work, maybe it's a 12-week camp. But, I knew that I was going up levels and levels, so I settled on a six-month training camp.

Figure 8.2 overleaf shows my half of the bathroom mirror six months out from the fight, much to Carly's disgust. This was what I called my 'ritual board', and there are a couple of things to point out. Right up in the top left, you'll see my goal: become a professional boxer. It's in a place where I see it every day, several times a day. You'll also see my 'why': authenticity. Being authentic is a deeply held value of mine, and I wanted to get into that ring as an authentic professional boxer – not someone who had turned 40 and was having a midlife crisis, or someone who wanted to tick off an item on a bucket list. It was really important that I was authentic, so I needed to really train my arse off. I hired an old-school boxing trainer called Bryce, and I went to train with him initially three times a week, then four, then five times as I built up my work volume. He was a real hard-arse, and I loved that about him.

Figure 8.2: My ritual board

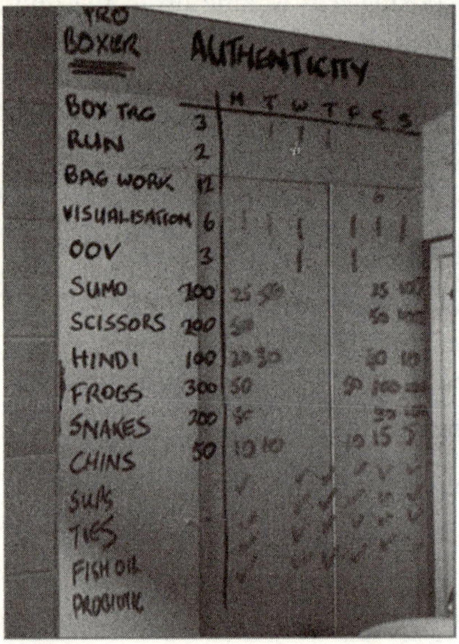

I incorporated lots of other rituals into my ritual board. I had things such as my visualisation (mental imagery) and going for a run a couple of times per week. Importantly, I had a bunch of 'instant rituals', which were things that I could do quickly and tick off my ritual board when I saw it. These were mostly bodyweight exercises and had names like 'scissors', 'sumo', 'frogs' and 'snakes'.

The names and exercises themselves are not important; it's the fact that they are easy to do when you see your ritual board that matters. I created a rule that every time I saw my mirror, I had to do something. What I discovered a few weeks into this process was that when I saw my mirror, did a ritual and ticked it off (or wrote the number that I did), my motivation seemed to increase. Success was breeding success.

That's when I had my big aha moment around motivation. I realised that most of us have got the motivation–action equation the wrong way around. Lots of us wait for the 'motivation fairy' to come along and wave it's magic 'motivation wand' to give us motivation to do something, but I realised through this process that it's the other way around…

Motivation follows action!

When I then thought about it from a neuroscience perspective, it was so bleeding obvious. There are a number of recognised natural rewards for the brain, such as food, water, sex, nurturing and achievement. When you receive these things, dopamine is released, which tells your brain, 'That felt good – do it again.' Dopamine is a neurotransmitter that's involved in pleasure and reward, but it's really the chemical of goal-directed behaviour, anticipation and motivation.

This was my epiphany, and I decided that I was going to gamify the ritual board. I wanted to see if I could increase my numbers in those body weight exercises every week. I thought about the Stoic philosopher Epictetus: 'Focus on what you can control, and refuse to invest your energy in that which you can't control'. I knew that my opponent was already an experienced professional boxer and that he was going to be more skilled and experienced. That sits in Epictetus's zone two: I can't control it. What I can control is the stuff in zone one: my fitness and my skills. So, that was where all my focus went, and those numbers started increasing every week.

To help this process, I created a heap of what I call 'if, then' behaviours.

- If the kettle is boiling, then I'm going to do frogs, and go and tick it off.
- If the TV is on and adverts are playing, then I'm going to do two minutes of exercise, and go and tick it off.

- If I go through my bedroom door, then I'm going to do 20 kick-sits, and go and tick it off.

I started creating habits out of all of these little movement snacks – 30 seconds here, 30 seconds there; a minute there, two minutes there. The numbers kept going up, and the gamification of trying to beat the week before was a huge motivator.

At the end of my camp, I was doing five sessions a week with my old-school boxing trainer. I was also doing my running, my visualisation and between 800 and 1000 of each one of those bodyweight exercises on top of my training. I ended up getting into the ring in exceptionally good shape, fitter than when I'd joined the military more than 20 years previously.

If you've ever done a boxing class, you'll know that hitting a punching bag tires you out pretty quickly. When stuff hits you back, it gets a lot more tiring a lot more quickly. You've also got a mouthguard in, which makes it a bit harder to breathe. Then, when your opponent breaks your nose in the third round of the fight, life becomes pretty challenging! I can now say without a shadow of a doubt that if I hadn't have been using the ritual board, there's no way that I would have ended up winning that fight.

We beat seven bells out of each other, he broke my nose, I split open his eye, and I ended up winning on points. Then we went to the after-party (both looking pretty horrible) and shared a few drinks and some mutual respect.

However, the point of this story is that the next day, Carly said, 'Get that off the bloody mirror', so I took it all off – and guess what happened? Everything went south. My exercise levels plummeted, and I realised that it was because, by removing the ritual board, I had lost both my trigger to do the rituals and my feedback mechanism – and with it, my motivation.

I then created a ritual board on an A4 whiteboard and hung it up in my kitchen. A couple of weeks later, my little girl, Ceara, who was seven at the time, said, 'Daddy, I want a ritual board'. So, we got Ceara a ritual board and hung it next to mine. Then my little boy, Oscar, who was only four, said, 'Daddy, I want a ritual board, too'. Now, ten years later, all four of us have ritual boards in the kitchen to help give us the motivation to do the behaviours we need to do.

I highly recommend that you get a ritual board and hang it somewhere where you will see it several times a day, be that in your kitchen, on your desk, on your bathroom mirror – wherever works for you. This will serve as both the trigger to do the behaviour and the feedback mechanism to enhance your motivation for further action. Motivation follows action.

Conclusion

I need to close now by giving you the bad news. This is not the way you're supposed to finish a book at all, but the realist in me tells me that I've got to give you the bad news. Here it is: no-one is coming, ever. Seriously. No-one's coming to short your shit out. They're just not. No-one's coming to make you awesome, to make you lose the weight, to get you in shape, to sort your head out, to make you a role model for your kids, or to help you achieve your life goals. They're just not coming, ever. This is all about you and the choices that you make every day. Are you going to stay mostly in your comfort zone and, ultimately, not achieve your true potential, or are you going to enter the world of ritual boards and experiments?

So, here's the experiment – get yourself a ritual board, and see what happens if you put a bunch of the rituals in this book onto the ritual board and then get up every morning and commit to a number of those rituals. Those rituals might include doing a short workout first thing in the morning, or choosing that 30-second cold shower even though you don't feel like it. Then you decide what version of you is going to be in control – your Inner Sage or your Inner Gremlin – and you consult your Sage when you're faced with challenges.

If you do this for four weeks, I guarantee you'll start to notice a positive impact on your physical and mental wellbeing – and if you do notice the impact, repeat the experiment.

Enjoy the journey.

About the author

A former British Royal Navy Aircrew Officer, Paul is an exercise physiologist, nutritionist and neuroscientist who is currently completing a PhD in applied psychology, where he is developing and testing resilience strategies with the Australian Defence Science Technology Group and the University of Newcastle.

He is the Director of The Mind-Body-Brain Performance Institute, through which he delivers resilience, leadership and executive performance workshops to a wide range of Australian and overseas corporations and the Australian Defence Force.

In 2010 Paul created and co-hosted the TV series *Body and Brain Overhaul*, and he appeared regularly on *The Biggest Loser* TV series as a subject-matter expert. In 2010 and 2015, he was voted Australian Fitness Industry Presenter of the Year.

Paul is the host of *The MindBodyBrain Project* podcast. His latest venture is The Mental Fitness Project, an online program and app that is currently being used by a number of corporations and has proven benefits for resilience, mental wellbeing and levels of burnout of participants.

Paul has a proven track record in leadership and dealing with high-pressure situations through his former roles as an Airborne Anti-submarine Warfare Officer and a Helicopter Search-and-rescue Crew Member with the Royal Navy Fleet Air Arm.

He has undergone rigorous military combat survival and resistance-to-interrogation training, and in 2012 he became a professional boxer. In 2019, he took up karate to create memories with his kids, and in 2021 both Paul and his 10-year-old son Oscar became Australian kumite champions.

About the author

References

Introduction

Australian Institute of Health and Welfare, 'Chronic disease', <aihw.gov.au/reports-data/health-conditions-disability-deaths/chronic-disease/overview>, accessed 6 September 2022.

FW Booth & PD Neufer, 'Exercise controls gene expression', *American Scientist*, vol. 93, January–February 2005, pp. 28–35.

FlowingData, 'History of Earth in 24-hour clock', 9 October 2012, <flowingdata.com/2012/10/09/history-of-earth-in-24-hour-clock/>.

WC Roberts, 'The Amish, body weight, and exercise', *The American Journal of Cardiology*, vol. 94, no. 9, November 2004, p. 1221.

M Starr, 'The history of life on Earth in a single day', CNET, 28 November 2012, <cnet.com/science/the-history-of-life-on-earth-in-a-single-day/>.

R Stelter, D de la Croix & M Myrskylä, 'Leaders and laggards in life expectancy among European scholars from the sixteenth to the early twentieth century', *Demography*, vol. 58, no. 1, 2021, pp. 111–135.

T Urban, 'Putting time in perspective – UPDATED', 22 August 2013, <waitbutwhy.com/2013/08/putting-time-in-perspective.html>.

Chapter 1: The good, the bad and the ugly of stress

Australian Psychological Society (APS), 'One-third of Australia stressed out', 8 November 2015, <psychology.org.au/news/media_releases/8nov2015-pw>.

PH Black, 'The inflammatory consequences of psychologic stress: relationship to insulin resistance, obesity, atherosclerosis and diabetes mellitus, type II', *Medical Hypotheses*, vol. 67, no. 4, 2006, pp. 879–891.

E Bourg & SIS Rattan (eds), *Mild Stress and Healthy Aging: Applying Hormesis in Aging Research and Interventions*, Springer Dordrecht, 2008.

E Calabrese, 'The dose–response revolution: how hormesis became significant: an historical and personal reflection', in SIS Rattan & M Kyriazis (eds), *The Science of Hormesis in Health and Longevity*, Academic Press, London, 2019.

M Csikszentmihalyi, *Flow: the psychology of optimal experience*, Harper Perennial Modern Classics, 2008.

A Damasio, *The feeling of what happens: body and emotion in the making of consciousness*, Harcourt Brace, New York, 1999.

D Furman, J Campisi, E Verdin, et al, 'Chronic inflammation in the etiology of disease across the life span', *Nature Medicine*, vol. 25, 2019, pp. 1822–1832.

AB Hains & AFT Arnsten, 'Molecular mechanisms of stress-induced prefrontal cortical impairment: implications for mental illness', *Learning & Memory*, vol. 15, no. 8, 2008, pp. 551–564.

AH Miller, V Maletic & CL Raison, 'Inflammation and its discontents: the role of cytokines in the pathophysiology of major depression', *Biological Psychiatry*, vol. 65, no. 9, May 2009, pp. 732–741.

EL O'Keefe, N Torres-Acosta, JH O'Keefe & CJ Lavie, 'Training for longevity: the reverse J-curve for exercise', *Missouri Medicine*, vol. 117, no. 4, July-August 2020, pp. 355–361.

A Vaiserman, 'Hormesis through low dose radiation', in SIS Rattan & M Kyriazis (eds), *The Science of Hormesis in Health and Longevity*, Academic Press, London, 2019.

D Vigo, G Thornicroft & R Atun, 'Estimating the true global burden of mental illness', *Lancet Psychiatry*, vol. 3, no. 2, February 2016, pp. 171–178.

World Health Organization, 'ICD-11: International Classification of Diseases 11th Revision: The global standard for diagnostic health information', <icd.who.int/en>, accessed 2 September 2022.

Chapter 2: Mobilise your metabolism

FW Booth & PD Neufer, op. cit.

E Burns & R Kakara, 'Deaths from falls among persons aged ≥65 years – United States, 2007–2016', *Morbidity and Mortality Weekly Report* (MMWR), vol. 67, no. 18, May 2018, pp. 509–514.

Centers for Disease Control and Prevention, 'General physical activities defined by level of intensity', <cdc.gov/nccdphp/dnpa/physical/pdf/pa_intensity_table_2_1.pdf>, accessed 6 September 2022.

TS Church, DM Thomas, C Tudor-Locke, et al, 'Trends over 5 decades in U.S. occupation-related physical activity and their associations with obesity', *PloS One*, vol. 6, no. 5, 2011.

AJ Crum & EJ Langer, 'Mind-set matters: exercise and the placebo effect', *Psychological Science*, vol. 18, no. 2, February 2007, pp. 165–171.

C Hoffmann & C Weigert, 'Skeletal muscle as an endocrine organ: the role of myokines in exercise adaptations', *Cold Spring Harbor Perspectives in Medicine*, vol. 7, no. 11, November 2017.

N Jones, '7 miles, 14,000 steps: keeping your heart healthy according to a study of postal workers', World Economic Forum, 7 March 2017, <weforum.org/agenda/2017/03/this-is-the-link-between-postal-workers-and-a-healthy-heart>.

JH Kwon, KM Moon & K-W Min, 'Exercise-induced myokines can explain the importance of physical activity in the elderly: an overview'. *Healthcare*, vol. 8, no. 4, 2020, p. 378.

H Momma, R Kawakami, T Honda & SS Sawada, 'Muscle-strengthening activities are associated with lower risk and mortality in major non-communicable diseases: a systematic review and meta-analysis of cohort studies', *British Journal of Sports Medicine*, vol. 56, 2022, pp. 755–763.

AJ Murray, 'Taking a HIT for the heart: why training intensity matters', *Journal of Applied Physiology*, vol. 111, no. 5, November 2011, pp. 1229–1230.

W Newman, G Parry-Williams, J Wiles, et al, 'Risk of atrial fibrillation in athletes: a systematic review and meta-analysis', *British Journal of Sports Medicine*, vol. 55, no. 21, pp. 1233–1238.

EL O'Keefe, N Torres-Acosta, JH O'Keefe & CJ Lavie, 'Training for longevity: the reverse J-curve for exercise', *Missouri Medicine*, vol. 117, no. 4, July–August 2020, pp. 355–361.

BK Pedersen & B Saltin, 'Exercise as medicine: evidence for prescribing exercise as therapy in 26 different chronic diseases', *Scandinavian Journal of Medicine and Science in Sports*, vol. 25, no. 3, November 2015, pp. 1–72.

DA Raichlen, H Pontzer, JA Harris, et al, 'Physical activity patterns and biomarkers of cardiovascular disease risk in hunter-gatherers', *American Journal of Human Biology*, vol. 29, no. 2, October 2016.

LJH Rasmussen, A Caspi, A Ambler, et al, 'Association of neurocognitive and physical function with gait speed in midlife', *JAMA Network Open*, vol. 2, no. 10, 2019.

PF Saint-Maurice, RP Troiano, DR Bassett Jr, et al, 'Association of daily step count and step intensity with mortality among US adults', *JAMA*, vol. 323, no. 12, 2020, pp. 1151–1160.

FB Schuch, D Vancampfort, J Richards, et al, 'Exercise as a treatment for depression: a meta-analysis adjusting for publication bias', *Journal of Psychiatric Research*, vol. 77, June 2016, pp. 42–51.

MCK Severinsen & BK Pedersen, 'Muscle-organ crosstalk: the emerging roles of myokines', *Endocrine Reviews*, vol. 41, no. 4, August 2020, pp. 594–609.

B Strasser & M Burtscher, 'Survival of the fittest: VO_2max, a key predictor of longevity?', *Frontiers in Bioscience-Landmark* (FBL), vol. 23, no. 8, 2018, pp. 1505–1516.

B Stubbs, D Vancampfort, S Rosenbaum, et al, 'An examination of the anxiolytic effects of exercise for people with anxiety and stress-related disorders: a meta-analysis', *Psychiatry Research*, vol. 249, March 2017, pp. 102–108.

HP van der Ploeg, T Chey, RJ Korda, et al, 'Sitting time and all-cause mortality risk in 222 497 Australian adults', *Archives of Internal Medicine*, vol. 172, no. 6, March 2012, pp. 494–500.

S Vaynman & F Gomez-Pinilla, 'Revenge of the "sit": how lifestyle impacts neuronal and cognitive health through molecular systems that interface energy metabolism with neuronal plasticity', *Journal of Neuroscience Research*, vol. 84, no. 4, September 2006, pp. 699–715.

E Volpi, R Nazemi & S Fujita, 'Muscle tissue changes with aging', *Current Opinion in Clinical Nutrition & Metabolic Care*, vol. 7, no. 4, July 2004, pp. 405–410.

BM Wood, JA Harris, DA Raichlen, et al, 'Gendered movement ecology and landscape use in Hadza hunter-gatherers', *Nature Human Behaviour*, vol. 5, 2021, pp. 436–446.

J Yao, N Lim, J Tan, et al, 'Evaluation of a population-wide mobile health physical activity program in 696 907 adults in Singapore', *Journal of the American Heart Association*, vol. 11, no. 12, June 2022.

Chapter 3: Harvest discomfort

GA Buijze, IN Sierevelt, BC van der Heijden, et al, 'The effect of cold showering on health and work: a randomized controlled trial', *PLoS One*, vol. 11, no. 9, September 2016.

JW Castellani & AJ Young, 'Human physiological responses to cold exposure: acute responses and acclimatization to prolonged exposure', *Autonomic Neuroscience*, vol. 196, April 2016, pp. 68–74.

CM Eglin & MJ Tipton, 'Repeated cold showers as a method of habituating humans to the initial responses to cold water immersion', *European Journal of Applied Physiology*, vol. 93, 2005, pp. 624–629.

E Ernst, E Pecho, P Wirz & T Saradeth, 'Regular sauna bathing and the incidence of common colds', *Annals of Medicine*, vol. 22, no. 4, 1990, pp. 225–227.

S Fujita, Y Ikeda, M Miyata, et al, 'Effect of Waon therapy on oxidative stress in chronic heart failure', *Circulation Journal*, vol. 75, no. 2, 2011, pp. 348–356.

A Garolla, M Torino, B Sartini, et al, 'Seminal and molecular evidence that sauna exposure affects human spermatogenesis', *Human Reproduction*, vol. 28, no. 4, April 2013, pp. 877–885.

JA Gill & MA La Merrill, 'An emerging role for epigenetic regulation of Pgc-1α expression in environmentally stimulated brown adipose thermogenesis', *Environmental Epigenetics*, vol. 3, no. 2, May 2017.

H Gravel, P Behzadi, S Cardinal, et al, 'Acute vascular benefits of Finnish sauna bathing in patients with stable coronary artery disease', *Canadian Journal of Cardiology*, vol. 37, no. 3, March 2021, pp. 493–499.

PS Hafen, CN Preece, JR Sorensen, et al, 'Repeated exposure to heat stress induces mitochondrial adaptation in human skeletal muscle', *Journal of Applied Physiology*, vol. 125, no. 5, November 2018, pp. 1447–1455.

ML Hannuksela & S Ellahham, 'Benefits and risks of sauna bathing', *The American Journal of Medicine*, vol. 110, no. 2, February 2001, pp. 118–126.

M Iguchi, AE Littmann, S-H Chang, et al, 'Heat stress and cardiovascular, hormonal, and heat shock proteins in humans', *Journal of Athletic Training*, vol. 47, no. 2, March/April 2012, pp. 184–190.

CW Janssen, CA Lowry, MR Mehl, et al, 'Whole-body hyperthermia for the treatment of major depressive disorder: a randomized clinical trial', *JAMA Psychiatry*, vol. 73, no. 8, 2016, pp. 789–795.

L Janský, D Pospíšilová, S Honzová, et al, 'Immune system of cold-exposed and cold-adapted humans', *European Journal of Applied Physiology and Occupational Physiology*, vol. 72, 1996, pp. 445–450.

DG Johnson, JS Hayward, TP Jacobs, et al, 'Plasma norepinephrine responses of man in cold water', *Journal of Applied Physiology*, vol. 43, no. 2, August 1977, pp. 216–220.

CM Judge, L Chasan-Taber, L Gensburg, et al, 'Physical exposures during pregnancy and congenital cardiovascular malformations', *Paediatric and Perinatal Epidemiology*, vol. 18, no. 5, September 2004, pp. 352–360.

K Kauppinen, 'Facts and fables about sauna', *Annals of the New York Academy of Sciences*, vol. 813, March 1997, pp. 654–662.

HU Klehr, S Goenechea & M Eichelbaum, 'Effect of extracorporeal hemoperfusion on the elimination of carbromal in carbromal poisoning', *Verhandlungen der Deutschen Gesellschaft fur Innere Medizin*, vol. 83, April 1977, pp. 1612–1614.

J Krop, 'Chemical sensitivity after intoxication at work with solvents: response to sauna therapy', *Journal of Alternative and Complementary Medicine*, vol. 4, no. 1, Spring 1998, pp. 77–86.

K Kukkonen-Harjula & K Kauppinen, 'Health effects and risks of sauna bathing', *International Journal of Circumpolar Health*, vol. 65, no. 3, 2006, pp. 195–205.

K Kukkonen-Harjula, P Oja, K Laustiola, et al, 'Haemodynamic and hormonal responses to heat exposure in a Finnish sauna bath', *European Journal of Applied Physiology and Occupational Physiology*, vol. 58, no. 5, 1989, pp. 543–550.

S Kuwahata, M Miyata, S Fujita, et al, 'Improvement of autonomic nervous activity by Waon therapy in patients with chronic heart failure', *Journal of Cardiology*, vol. 57, no. 1, 2011, pp. 100–106.

LA Laitinen, A Lindqvist & M Heino, 'Lungs and ventilation in sauna', *Annals of Clinical Research*, vol. 20, no. 4, 1988, pp. 244–248.

T Laukkanen, H Khan, F Zaccardi & JA Laukkanen, 'Association between sauna bathing and fatal cardiovascular and all-cause mortality events', *JAMA Internal Medicine*, vol. 175, no. 4, 2015, pp. 542–548.

T Laukkanen, S Kunutsor, J Kauhanen & JA Laukkanen, 'Sauna bathing is inversely associated with dementia and Alzheimer's disease in middle-aged Finnish men', *Age and Ageing*, vol. 46, no. 2, December 2016, pp. 245–249.

RK Leak, 'Heat shock proteins in neurodegenerative disorders and aging', *Journal of Cell Communication and Signaling*, vol. 8, no. 4, December 2014, pp. 293–310.

JA Lindquist & PR Mertens, 'Cold shock proteins: from cellular mechanisms to pathophysiology and disease', *Cell Communication and Signaling*, vol. 16, 2018.

R Livingston, 'Medical risks and benefits of the sweat lodge', *Journal of Alternative and Complementary Medicine*, vol. 16, no. 6, June 2010, pp. 617–619.

A Masuda, M Miyata, T Kinata, et al, 'Repeated sauna therapy reduces urinary 8-epi-prostaglandin F(2alpha)', *Japanese Heart Journal*, vol. 45, no. 2, March 2004, pp. 297–303.

A Matsuda, M Nakazato, T Kihara, et al, 'Repeated thermal therapy diminishes appetite loss and subjective complaints in mildly depressed patients', *Psychosomatic Medicine*, vol. 67, no. 4, July–August 2005, pp. 643–647.

K Matsushita, A Masuda & C Tei, 'Efficacy of Waon therapy for fibromyalgia', *Internal Medicine*, vol. 47, no. 16, 2008, pp. 1473–1476.

MF McCarty, J Barroso-Aranda & F Contreras, 'Regular thermal therapy may promote insulin sensitivity while boosting expression of endothelial nitric oxide synthase – effects comparable to those of exercise training', *Medical Hypotheses*, vol. 73, no. 1, July 2009, pp. 103–105.

T Ohori, T Nozawa, H ihori, et al, 'Effect of repeated sauna treatment on exercise tolerance and endothelial function in patients with chronic heart failure', *The American Journal of Cardiology*, vol. 109, no. 1, January 2012, pp. 100–104.

RP Patrick & TL Johnson, 'Sauna use as a lifestyle practice to extend healthspan', *Experimental Gerontology*, vol. 154, October 2021.

W Pilch, I Pokora, Z Szyguła, et al, 'Effect of a single Finnish sauna session on white blood cell profile and cortisol levels in athletes and non-athletes', *Journal of Human Kinetics*, vol. 39, December 2013, pp. 127–135.

W Pilch, Z Szygula, T Palka, et al, 'Comparison of physiological reactions and physiological strain in healthy men under heat stress in dry and steam heat saunas', *Biology of Sport*, vol. 31, no. 2, 2014, pp. 145–149.

GH Ross & MC Sternquist, 'Methamphetamine exposure and chronic illness in police officers: significant improvement with sauna-based detoxification therapy', *Toxicology and Industrial Health*, vol. 28, no. 8, September 2012, pp. 758–768.

NA Shevchuk, 'Adapted cold shower as a potential treatment for depression', *Medical Hypotheses*, vol. 70, no. 5, 2008, pp. 995–1001.

Y Soejima, T Munemoto, A Masuda, et al, 'Effects of Waon therapy on chronic fatigue syndrome: a pilot study', *Internal Medicine*, vol. 54, no. 3, 2015, pp. 333–338.

MJ Tipton, FSC Golden, C Higenbottam, et al, 'Temperature dependence of habituation of the initial responses to cold-water immersion', *European Journal of Applied Physiology and Occupational Physiology*, vol. 78, 1998, pp. 253–257.

MM Toner & WD McArdle, 'Human thermoregulatory responses to acute cold stress with special reference to water immersion', *Comprehensive Physiology*, 2011.

K Wähä-Eskeli & R Erkkola, 'The sauna and pregnancy', *Annals of Clinical Research*, vol. 20, no. 4, 1988, pp. 279–282.

RPA Wallin, A Lundqvist, SH Moré, et al, 'Heat-shock proteins as activators of the innate immune system', *Trends in Immunology*, vol. 23, no. 3, March 2002, pp. 130–135.

Chapter 4. Fuel your ecosystem

M Adjibade, C Julia, B Allès, et al, 'Prospective association between ultra-processed food consumption and incident depressive symptoms in the French NutriNet-Santé cohort', *BMC Medicine*, vol. 17, no. 78, 2019.

M Albosta & J Bakke, 'Intermittent fasting: is there a role in the treatment of diabetes? A review of the literature and guide for primary care physicians', *Clinical Diabetes and Endocrinology*, vol. 7, no. 3, 2021.

RK Amaravadi, AC Kimmelman & J Debnath, 'Targeting autophagy in cancer: recent advances and future directions', *Cancer Discovery*, vol. 9, no. 9, 2019, pp. 1167–1181.

M Bagherniya, AE Butler, GE Barreto & A Sahebkar, 'The effect of fasting or calorie restriction on autophagy induction: a review of the literature', *Ageing Research Reviews*, vol. 47, November 2018, pp. 183–197.

P Baker, P Machado, T Santos, et al, 'Ultra-processed foods and the nutrition transition: global, regional and national trends, food systems transformations and political economy drivers', *Obesity Reviews*, vol. 21, no. 12, August 2020.

T Bar-Yosef, O Damri & G Agam, 'Dual role of autophagy in diseases of the central nervous system', *Frontiers in Cellular Neuroscience*, vol. 13, p. 196.

S Brandhorst, IY Choi, M Wei, et al, 'A periodic diet that mimics fasting promotes multi-system regeneration, enhanced cognitive performance, and healthspan', *Cell Metabolism*, vol. 22, no. 1, July 2015, pp. 86–99.

S Brandhorst & VD Longo, 'Fasting and caloric restriction in cancer prevention and treatment', *Metabolism in Cancer*, vol. 207, 2016, pp. 241–266.

S Camandola & MP Mattson, 'Brain metabolism in health, aging, and neurodegeneration', *The EMBO Journal*, vol. 36, no. 11, June 2017, pp. 1474–1492.

A Chaix, ENC Manoogian, GC Melkani & S Panda, 'Time-restricted eating to prevent and manage chronic metabolic diseases', *Annual Review of Nutrition*, vol. 39, August 2019, pp. 291–315.

X Chen, Z Zhang, H Yang, et al, 'Consumption of ultra-processed foods and health outcomes: a systematic review of epidemiological studies', *Nutrition Journal*, vol. 19, no. 86, 2020.

C-W Cheng, V Villani, R Buono, et al, 'Fasting-mimicking diet promotes Ngn3-driven β-cell regeneration to reverse diabetes', *Cell*, vol. 168, no. 5, February 2017, pp. 775–788.

I Y Choi, L Piccio, P Childress, et al, 'A diet mimicking fasting promotes regeneration and reduces autoimmunity and multiple sclerosis symptoms', *Cell Reports*, vol. 15, no. 10, June 2016, pp. 2136–2146.

RJ Colman, RM Anderson, SC Johnson, et al, 'Caloric restriction delays disease onset and mortality in rhesus monkeys', *Science*, vol. 325, no. 5937, July 2009, pp. 201–204.

M Demasi, 'Dietitians backslide – dump corporate sponsorships, invite ads instead', *Michael West Media*, 17 May 2019, <michaelwest.com.au/dietitians-backslide-dump-corporate-sponsorships-invite-ads-instead/>.

M Demasi, 'Kellogg's "junk science" and Australia's health policy', *Michael West Media*, 7 December 2017, <michaelwest.com.au/kelloggs-junk-science-and-australias-health-policy/>.

M Demasi, 'Vindication: dietitians cut ties with sugar lobby', *Michael West Media*, 6 October 2018, <michaelwest.com.au/vindication-dietitians-cut-ties-with-sugar-lobby/>.

L Elizabeth, P Machado, M Zinöcker, et al, 'Ultra-processed foods and health outcomes: a narrative review', *Nutrients*, vol. 12, no. 7, June 2020, p. 1955.

T Fiolet, B Srour, L Sellem, et al, 'Consumption of ultra-processed foods and cancer risk: results from NutriNet-Santé prospective cohort', *BMJ*, vol. 360, 2018.

L Fontana & L Partridge, 'Promoting health and longevity through diet: from model organisms to humans', *Cell*, vol. 161, no. 1, March 2015, pp. 106–118.

K Giannakou, C Papakonstantinou, S Chrysostomou & D Lamnisos, 'The effect of intermittent fasting on cancer prevention: a systematic review', *European Journal of Public Health*, vol. 30, no. 5, September 2020.

S Greenhalgh, J King & WC Fairbank, 'Making China safe for Coke: how Coca-Cola shaped obesity science and policy in China', *BMJ*, vol. 364, 2019.

S de Groot, H Pijl, JJM van der Hoeven & JR Kroep, 'Effects of short-term fasting on cancer treatment', *Journal of Experimental & Clinical Cancer Research*, vol. 38, 2019.

ILSI Global, <ilsi.org>, accessed 1 September 2022.

KD Hall, A Ayuketah, R Brychta, et al, 'Ultra-processed diets cause excess calorie intake and weight gain: an inpatient randomized controlled trial of ad libitum food intake', *Cell Metabolism*, vol. 30, no. 1, July 2019, pp. 67–77.

Z Harcombe, JS Baker, SM Cooper, et al, 'Evidence from randomised controlled trials did not support the introduction of dietary fat guidelines in 1977 and 1983: a systematic review and meta-analysis', *Open Heart*, vol. 2, no. 1, January 2015.

MN Harvie, M Pegington, MP Mattson, et al, 'The effects of intermittent or continuous energy restriction on weight loss and metabolic disease risk markers: a randomized trial in young overweight women', *International Journal of Obesity*, vol. 35, no. 5, May 2011, pp. 714–727.

RF Houser & G Baghdady, 'Sugar consumption in the US diet between 1822 and 2005', *Online Statistics Education: An Interactive Multimedia Course of Study*, <onlinestatbook.com/2/case_studies/sugar.html>, accessed 6 September 2022.

FN Jacka, A O'Neil, R Opie, et al, 'A randomised controlled trial of dietary improvement for adults with major depression (the "SMILES" trial)', *BMC Medicine*, vol. 15, no. 1, January 2017, p. 23.

A Jacobs, 'A shadowy industry group shapes food policy around the world', *The New York Times*, 16 September 2019, <nytimes.com/2019/09/16/health/ilsi-food-policy-india-brazil-china.html>.

H Jamshed, RA Beyl, DL Della Manna, et al, 'Early time-restricted feeding improves 24-hour glucose levels and affects markers of the circadian clock, aging, and autophagy in humans', *Nutrients*, vol. 11, no. 6, June 2019, p. 1234.

JB Johnson, W Summer, RG Cutler, et al, 'Alternate day calorie restriction improves clinical findings and reduces markers of oxidative stress and inflammation in overweight adults with moderate asthma', *Free Radical Biology & Medicine*, vol. 42, no. 5, March 2007, pp. 665–674.

E Kwong, J Williams, P Baker, et al, 'How big companies are targeting middle income countries to boost ultra-processed food sales', *The Conversation*, 14 September 2021, <theconversation.com/how-big-companies-are-targeting-middle-income-countries-to-boost-ultra-processed-food-sales-166927>.

F Laudisi, C Stolfi & G Monteleone, 'Impact of food additives on gut homeostasis', *Nutrients*, vol. 11, no. 10, October 2019, p. 2334.

RH Liu, 'Health-promoting components of fruits and vegetables in the diet', *Advances in Nutrition*, vol. 4, no. 3, May 2013, pp. 384S–392S.

VD Longo & MP Mattson, 'Fasting: molecular mechanisms and clinical applications', *Cell Metabolism*, vol. 19, no. 2, February 2014, pp. 181–192.

J Martel, DM Ojcius, Y-F Ko, et al, 'Hormetic effects of phytochemicals on health and longevity', *Trends in Endocrinology and Metabolism*, vol. 30, no. 6, June 2019, pp. 335–346.

MP Mattson, 'Energy intake and exercise as determinants of brain health and vulnerability to injury and disease', *Cell Metabolism*, vol. 16, no. 6, December 2012 pp. 706–722.

MP Mattson, 'Challenging oneself intermittently to improve health', *Dose Response*, vol. 12, no. 4, October 2014, pp. 600–618.

MP Mattson, W Duan, R Wan & Z Guo, 'Prophylactic activation of neuroprotective stress response pathways by dietary and behavioral manipulations', *NeuroRx*, vol. 1, no. 1, January 2004, pp. 111–116.

P Mejia, JH Trevino-Villarreal, C Hine, et al, 'Dietary restriction protects against experimental cerebral malaria via leptin modulation and T-cell mTORC1 suppression', *Nature Communications*, vol. 6, January 2015, p. 6050.

JR Mitchell, M Verweij, K Brand, et al, 'Short-term dietary restriction and fasting precondition against ischemia reperfusion injury in mice', *Aging Cell*, vol. 9, no. 1, February 2010, pp. 40–53.

CA Monteiro, J-C Moubarac, G Cannon, et al, 'Ultra-processed products are becoming dominant in the global food system', *Obesity Reviews*, vol. 14, no. 2, November 2013, pp. 21–28.

K Pallauf & G Rimbach, 'Autophagy, polyphenols and healthy ageing', *Ageing Research Reviews*, vol. 12, no. 1, January 2013, pp. 237–252.

P Rangan, I Choi, M Wei, et al, 'Fasting-mimicking diet modulates microbiota and promotes intestinal regeneration to reduce inflammatory bowel disease pathology', *Cell Reports*, vol. 26, no. 10, March 2019, pp. 2704–2719.

F Rauber, E Martínez Steele, ML da Costa Louzada, et al, 'Ultra-processed food consumption and indicators of obesity in the United Kingdom population (2008-2016)', *PLoS One*, vol. 15, no. 5, 2020.

E Ravussin, LM Redman, J Rochon, et al, 'A 2-year randomized controlled trial of human caloric restriction: feasibility and effects on predictors of health span and longevity', *The Journals of Gerontology. Series A, Biological Sciences and Medical Sciences*, vol. 70, no. 9, September 2015, pp. 1097–1104.

A Rico-Campà, MA Martínez-González, I Alvarez-Alvarez, et al, 'Association between consumption of ultra-processed foods and all cause mortality: SUN prospective cohort study', *BMJ*, vol. 365, 2019.

S Rosas-Plaza, A Hernández-Terán, M Navarro-Díaz, et al, 'Human gut microbiome across different lifestyles: from hunter-gatherers to urban populations', *Frontiers in Microbiology*, vol. 13, April 2022.

CA Rynders, EA Thomas, A Zaman, et al, 'Effectiveness of intermittent fasting and time-restricted feeding compared to continuous energy restriction for weight loss', *Nutrients*, vol. 11, no. 10, October 2019, p. 2442.

AMJ Sanchez, H Bernardi, G Py & R Candau, 'Autophagy is essential to support skeletal muscle plasticity in response to endurance exercise', *AJP Regulatory Integrative and Comparative Physiology*, vol. 307, no. 8, pp. R956–R969.

B Srour, LK Fezeu, E Kesse-Guyot, et al, 'Ultra-processed food intake and risk of cardiovascular disease: prospective cohort study (NutriNet-Santé)', *BMJ*, 365, 2019.

University of California, San Francisco (UCSF), 'Industry Documents Library', <industrydocuments.ucsf.edu>, accessed 1 September 2022.

C Valenti, 'Kraft's Philip Morris Connection', *ABC News*, 13 June 2001, <abcnews.go.com/Business/story?id=88088>.

HC Wastyk, GK Fragiadakis, D Perelman, et al, 'Gut-microbiota-targeted diets modulate human immune status', *Cell*, vol. 184, no. 16, August 2021, pp. 4137–4153.

L Yang, D Licastro, E Cava, et al, 'Long-term calorie restriction enhances cellular quality-control processes in human skeletal muscle', *Cell Reports*, vol. 14, no. 3, January 2016, pp. 422–428.

L Zheng, J Sun, X Yu & D Zhang, 'Ultra-processed food is positively associated with depressive symptoms among United States adults', *Frontiers in Nutrition*, vol. 7, December 2020.

Chapter 5. Sculpt your brain

D Goleman, *Emotional Intelligence*, Bantam Books, 2007.

VE Frankl, *Man's search for meaning: an introduction to logotherapy*, Beacon Press, Boston, 1962.

HistoryNet, 'Vice Admiral James Bond Stockdale: Vietnam War hero and indomitable spirit at the Hanoi Hilton', 18 July 2006, <historynet.com/vice-admiral-james-bond-stockdale-vietnam-war-hero-and-indomitable-spirit-at-the-hanoi-hilton/>.

A Pascual-Leone, D Nguyet, LG Cohen, et al, 'Modulation of muscle responses evoked by transcranial magnetic stimulation during the acquisition of new fine motor skills', *Journal of Neurophysiology*, vol. 74, no. 3, October 1995, pp. 1037–1045.

JB Stockdale, *Courage under fire: testing Epictetus's doctrines in a laboratory of human behaviour*, Hoover Institution, Stanford University, Stanford, CA, 1993.

What the Bleep Do we Know!?, motion picture, 2004.

Chapter 6. Recover and regenerate

PK Alvaro, RM Roberts & JK Harris, 'A systematic review assessing bidirectionality between sleep disturbances, anxiety, and depression', *Sleep*, vol. 36, no. 7, July 2013, pp. 1059–1068.

D Hale & K Marshall, 'Sleep and sleep hygiene', *Home Healthcare Now*, vol. 37, no. 4, July/August 2019, p. 227.

SI Hopper, SL Murray, LR Ferrara & JK Singleton, 'Effectiveness of diaphragmatic breathing for reducing physiological and psychological stress in adults: a quantitative systematic review', *JBI Database of Systematic Reviews and Implementation Reports*, vol. 17, no. 9, September 2019, pp. 1855–1876.

M Knufinke, A Nieuwenhuys, SAE Geurts, et al, 'Self-reported sleep quantity, quality and sleep hygiene in elite athletes', *Journal of Sleep Research*, vol. 27, no. 1, February 2018, pp. 78–85.

J Lowrie & H Brownlow, 'The impact of sleep deprivation and alcohol on driving: a comparative study', *BMC Public Health*, vol. 20, no. 980, 2020.

P Meerlo, A Sgoifo & D Suchecki, 'Restricted and disrupted sleep: effects on autonomic function, neuroendocrine stress systems and stress responsivity', *Sleep Medicine Reviews*, vol. 12, no. 3, June 2008, pp. 197–210.

C Newport, *Deep work: rules for focused success in a distracted world*, Grand Central Publishing; New York, 2016.

TF Robles & JE Carroll, 'Restorative biological processes and health', *Social and Personality Psychology Compass*, vol. 5, no. 8, August 2001, pp. 518–537.

LD Salay, N Ishiko & AD Huberman, 'A midline thalamic circuit determines reactions to visual threat', *Nature*, vol. 557, May 2018, pp. 183–189.

H Selänne & Juhani Leppäluoto, 'Common traits in overtrained athletes and in persons with professional burn-out', *Athletic Insight*, vol. 5, no. 3, February 2001, pp. 661–666.

S Taheri, L Lin, D Austin, et al, 'Short sleep duration is associated with reduced leptin, elevated ghrelin, and increased body mass index'. *PLoS Medicine*, vol. 1, no. 3, December 2004.

R Wassing, O Lakbila-Kamal, JR Ramautar, et al, 'Restless REM sleep impedes overnight amygdala adaptation', *Current Biology*, vol. 29, July 2019, pp. 2351–2358.

W Zhang, K Piotrowska, B Chavoshan, et al, 'Sleep duration is associated with testis size in healthy young men', *Journal of Clinical Sleep Medicine*, vol. 14, no. 10, October 2018, pp. 1757–1764.

Chapter 7. Connect through the power of the tap code

E Abi-Jaoude, KT Naylor & A Pignatiello, 'Smartphones, social media use and youth mental health'; *Canadian Medical Association Journal*, vol. 192, no. 6, February 2020, pp. E136–E141.

Big Think, 'Dennis Charney: resilience lessons from our veterans', video, YouTube, 30 October 2012, <youtube.com/watch?v=XoN1pv2JKpc >.

B Brown, 'The power of vulnerability', video, TED <ted.com/talks/brene_brown_the_power_of_vulnerability>, accessed 1 September 2022.

D Buettner, *The Blue Zones Challenge: A 4-Week Plan for a Longer, Better Life*, National Geographic Society, 2022.

L Ellis, *Leading with honor: leadership lessons from the Hanoi Hilton*, Freedom Star Media, 2012.

JH Fowler & NA Christakis, 'Dynamic spread of happiness in a large social network: longitudinal analysis over 20 years in the Framingham Heart Study', *BMJ*, vol. 337, 2008.

P Fretwell, TB Kiland & JP London, *Lessons from the Hanoi Hilton: six characteristics of high performance teams*. Naval Institute Press, Annapolis, MD, 2013.

S Misra, L Cheng, J Genevie & M Yuan, 'The iPhone effect: the quality of in-personal social interactions in the presence of mobile devices', *Environment and Behavior*, vol. 48, no. 2, July 2014, pp. 275–298.

The Economist, 'How heavy use of social media is linked to mental illness', 18 May 2018, <economist.com/graphic-detail/2018/05/18/how-heavy-use-of-social-media-is-linked-to-mental-illness>.

Chapter 8. Make the shift

FB Gillison, P Rouse, M Standage, et al, 'A meta-analysis of techniques to promote motivation for health behaviour change from a self-determination theory perspective', *Health Psychology Review*, vol. 13, no. 1, 2019, pp. 110–130.

D Hardy, *The compound effect: jumpstart your income, your life, your success*, Hachette Books, 2020.

AE Kelley & KC Berridge, 'The neuroscience of natural rewards: relevance to addictive drugs', *The Journal of Neuroscience*, vol. 22, no. 9, May 2002, pp. 3306–3311.

L Solbrig, B Whalley, DJ Kavanagh, et al, 'Functional imagery training versus motivational interviewing for weight loss: a randomised controlled trial of brief individual interventions for overweight and obesity', *International Journal of Obesity*, vol. 43, 2019, pp. 883–894.

The Center for Self-Determination Theory (CSDT), 'The Theory', <selfdeterminationtheory.org/the-theory/>, accessed 6 September 2022.

Index